Malcolm X Talks
to Young People

D1111780

Malcolm X
TALKS TO
YOUNG PEOPLE

*Speeches in the United States,
Britain, and Africa*

Pathfinder

NEW YORK   LONDON   MONTREAL   SYDNEY

Edited by Steve Clark

ISBN 0-87348-962-4
Library of Congress Catalog Card No. 90-64197
Manufactured in the United States of America

First edition, 1991
Second edition, 2002

Cover design by Eric Simpson
Cover portrait by Carole Byard, from the Pathfinder Mural
Photo by Margrethe Siem

Pathfinder

410 West Street, New York, NY 10014, U.S.A.
www.pathfinderpress.com
E-mail: pathfinderpress@compuserve.com
Fax: (212) 727-0150

PATHFINDER DISTRIBUTORS AROUND THE WORLD:
Australia (and Southeast Asia and the Pacific):
    Pathfinder, Level 1, 3/281-287 Beamish St., Campsie, NSW 2194
    Postal address: P.O. Box 164, Campsie, NSW 2194
Canada:
    Pathfinder, 2761 Dundas St. West, Toronto, ON, M6P 1Y4
Iceland:
    Pathfinder, Skolavordustig 6B, Reykjavík
    Postal address: P. Box 0233, IS 121 Reykjavík
New Zealand:
    Postal address: P.O. Box 3025, Auckland
Sweden:
    Pathfinder, Domargränd 16, S-129 47 Hägersten
United Kingdom (and Europe, Africa, Middle East, and South Asia):
    Pathfinder, 47 The Cut, London, SE1 8LL
United States (and Caribbean, Latin America, and East Asia):
    Pathfinder, 410 West Street, New York, NY 10014

CONTENTS

PREFACE

Malcolm X seized every occasion to talk with young people. All over the world, it is young people "who are actually involving themselves in the struggle to eliminate oppression and exploitation," he said in January 1965, responding to a question from a young socialist leader in the United States.

They "are the ones who most quickly identify with the struggle and the necessity to eliminate the evil conditions that exist. And here in this country," he emphasized, "it has been my observation that when you get into a conversation on racism and discrimination and segregation, you will find young people more incensed over it—they feel more filled with an urge to eliminate it."

This conviction about the receptivity of youth to a revolutionary message runs throughout the four talks and the interview presented in this expanded second edition of *Malcolm X Talks to Young People.* This new edition includes material by Malcolm never before in print, a 1966 tribute to the revolutionary leader, as well as an expanded display of photographs. It is being produced together with a first-ever Spanish-language edition, entitled *Malcolm X habla a la juventud,* which is being released simultaneously by Pathfinder Press and by Casa Editora Abril, the publishing house of the Union of Young Communists in Cuba. *Malcolm X Talks to Young People* was first published in 1965 as a Young Socialist pamphlet, and then enlarged into a book in 1991.

Malcolm X was born Malcolm Little on May 19, 1925, in Omaha, Nebraska. His father, a Baptist minister, was a follower of Marcus Garvey's back-to-Africa movement, the Universal

Negro Improvement Association. His mother was originally from the Caribbean nation of Grenada. When Malcolm was six, after his family had moved to Lansing, Michigan, his father was murdered by a racist gang.

As a teenager Malcolm lived in Boston and New York, where he got involved in petty crime. In 1946 he was arrested and convicted on burglary charges, spending six years in a Massachusetts state prison. It was while behind bars that Malcolm began reading voraciously—world history, philosophy, language, science, literature, whatever he could find in the prison library. And it was there that he developed the attributes—confidence in his own self-worth, the discipline for hard work and concentrated study—that were the foundation stones of his later transformation into a revolutionary political leader.

Malcolm's conversion to the Nation of Islam while in jail was not a political act, nor simply a religious one, in the way those terms are normally understood. It was the particular road along which he pulled his life back together, and became Malcolm X, after living for several years as a street hustler and small-time criminal. In his autobiography, he recounts unflinchingly "how deeply the religion of Islam had reached down into the mud to lift me up, to save me from being what I inevitably would have been: a dead criminal in a grave, or, if still alive, a flint-hard, bitter, thirty-seven-year-old convict in some penitentiary, or insane asylum."

After being paroled in 1952, Malcolm was soon appointed by Nation leader Elijah Muhammad as one of its ministers, taking the name Malcolm X. He later served as editor of the Nation's newspaper, its national spokesman, and head of its largest unit, New York City's Mosque no. 7 in Harlem. By the opening of the 1960s, Malcolm was politically drawn more and more toward the rising struggles by Blacks and other oppressed peoples in the United States and around the world. He used his platforms in Harlem and Black neighborhoods across the country, as well as on dozens of college campuses, to denounce the policies of the U.S. government both at home and abroad. He campaigned against every manifestation of anti-Black racism and was outspoken in condemning the pillage and oppression of the peoples of Africa, Asia, and Latin America for the profit and power of the U.S. and other imperialist regimes.

"The black revolution is sweeping Asia, is sweeping Africa, is rearing its head in Latin America," Malcolm said in a November 1963 talk to a predominantly Black audience in Detroit. "The Cuban Revolution—that's a revolution," he continued. "They overturned the system. Revolution is in Asia, revolution is in Africa, and the white man is screaming because he sees revolution in Latin America. How do you think he'll react to you when you learn what a real revolution is?"

By 1962 it was becoming more and more noticeable that Malcolm was straining against the narrow perspectives of the Nation of Islam, a bourgeois nationalist organization with a leadership bent on finding a separate economic niche for itself within the U.S. capitalist system. He described these growing tensions in a New Year's Day 1965 talk to a group of high-school age civil rights militants from McComb, Mississippi, which is included in this book. The Nation's hierarchy, Malcolm said, blocked any initiatives by him or others to carry out "militant action, uncompromising action." In April 1962, for example, Elijah Muhammad ordered Malcolm to call off street actions he was organizing in Los Angeles to protest the killing of Nation member Ronald Stokes and the wounding of six other Muslims by city cops.

The conflicts that led to Malcolm being forced out of the Nation of Islam came to a head in 1963. In April Malcolm was called by Elijah Muhammad to his winter home in Phoenix, Arizona. There Malcolm learned from the Nation leader himself the truth of rumors then spreading in the organization that Muhammad had engaged in sexual relations with a number of young women belonging to the Nation of Islam then working as staff members. Several of them had become pregnant, and Muhammad had taken advantage of his authority in the Nation to have them subjected to humiliating internal trials and suspended from membership for "fornication."

Coming on top of Malcolm's growing political clashes with the Nation hierarchy, the discovery of this corrupt and hypocritical behavior marked a turning point. "I felt the movement was dragging its feet in many areas," Malcolm said in a January 1965 interview with the *Young Socialist* magazine, printed here. "It didn't involve itself in the civil or civic or political struggles our people were confronted by. All it did was stress the importance of moral reformation—don't drink, don't smoke, don't permit fornication and adultery. When I found that the hierarchy itself wasn't practicing what it preached, it was clear that this part of its program was bankrupt."

In early March 1964, Malcolm announced his decision to break with the Nation of Islam. He and his collaborators initially organized themselves as the Muslim Mosque, Inc. But as Malcolm explained to the youth from McComb, Mississippi, he soon recognized that "there was a problem confronting our people in this country that had nothing to do with religion and went above and beyond religion"—a problem that, because of its magnitude, "a religious organization couldn't attack." So in June he initiated the formation of "another group that had nothing to do with religion whatsoever"—the Organization of Afro-American Unity (OAAU), open to all Blacks committed to Malcolm's revolutionary social and political trajectory.

During the final months of 1964 and early 1965, Malcolm won an increasingly wide hearing, not just across the United States but also on several continents among youth and other militants of various races and beliefs. He made two extensive trips to Africa and the Middle East, several short trips to Europe, and had scheduled more. One of the four talks in this collection was given in Africa and two in the United Kingdom.

The U.S. government took notice of the increased standing Malcolm was winning worldwide among radicalizing youth and workers. Previously classified government records released in the late 1970s confirm that the FBI had carried out systematic surveillance of him starting in 1953, shortly after he became a minister of the Nation of Islam. But this spying and harassment intensified, both in the United States and during his trips abroad, after Malcolm's break with the Nation and founding of the OAAU. Moreover, declassified records of the FBI's Counterintelligence Program (Cointelpro) document how the FBI used agents provocateurs to exacerbate murderous conflicts between groups involved in the Black liberation movement.

During the last year of his life, Malcolm X spoke out more and more directly about the capitalist roots of racism, of exploitation, and of imperialist oppression. Malcolm never gave an inch to U.S. patriotism, let alone imperialist nationalism. Blacks in the United States are "the victims of Americanism," he said in his May 1964 talk at the University of Ghana, printed here.

Malcolm was an uncompromising opponent of the Democratic and Republican parties—the twin parties of racism and capitalist exploitation. Malcolm urged the McComb, Mississippi, youth not to "run around . . . trying to make friends with somebody who's depriving you of your rights. They're not your friends. No, they're your enemies. Treat them like that and fight them, and you'll get your freedom. And after you get your freedom, your enemy will respect you."

In 1964 Malcolm refused to endorse or campaign for Democratic presidential candidate Lyndon Baines Johnson against Republican Barry Goldwater. "The Democratic Party is responsible for the racism that exists in this country, along with the Republican Party," he said in the *Young Socialist* interview. "The leading racists in this country are Democrats. Goldwater isn't the leading racist—he's a racist but not the leading racist. . . . If you check, whenever any kind of legislation is suggested to mitigate the injustices that Negroes suffer in this country, you will find that the people who line up against it are members of Lyndon B. Johnson's party." It was also the Johnson administration, Malcolm often pointed out, that was presiding over the U.S. war against the people of Vietnam and the slaughter of liberation fighters and villagers in the Congo. The revolutionary integrity underlying this political intransigence in the 1964 elections set Malcolm apart from, and helped earn him the enmity of, just about every other leader of prominent Black rights organizations or the trade unions, as well as the vast majority of those who called themselves radicals, Socialists, or Communists.

Malcolm X stretched out his hand to revolutionaries and freedom fighters in Africa, the Middle East, Asia, and elsewhere. In December 1964 Malcolm, who had demonstratively welcomed Fidel Castro to Harlem four years earlier, invited Cuban revolutionary leader Ernesto Che Guevara to speak before an OAAU meeting in Harlem. At the last minute Guevara was unable to attend but sent "the warm salutations of the Cuban people" to the meeting in a message that Malcolm insisted on reading himself from the platform.

On February 21, 1965—ten days after the final talk in this collection, presented at the London School of Economics— Malcolm X was assassinated. He was shot as he began speaking to an OAAU meeting at the Audubon Ballroom in Harlem. The following year three men, all members or supporters of the Nation of Islam, were convicted of the murder and each given a twenty-year-to-life sentence. One of them, the gunman arrested at the scene, had said from the outset that the two men convicted along with him were not guilty. In 1977 he signed affidavits stating that four other Nation supporters were the ones involved with him, but the case has never been reopened.

As the interview and talks in these pages show, Malcolm

came to recognize that what ties fighters against oppression and exploitation together is their shared revolutionary convictions, commitment, and deeds, not the color of their skin. When he spoke in December 1964 at Oxford University in the United Kingdom, Malcolm ended his presentation, printed here, by saying: "The young generation of whites, Blacks, browns, whatever else there is, you're living at a time of extremism, a time of revolution, a time when there's got to be a change. People in power have misused it. . . . And I for one will join in with anyone, I don't care what color you are, as long as you want to change this miserable condition that exists on this earth."

In the United States, Malcolm X spoke on three occasions—in April and May 1964, and again in January 1965—to large meetings of the Militant Labor Forum in New York City organized by supporters of the revolutionary socialist newsweekly, *The Militant.* This was a departure for Malcolm. Even while still a spokesperson for the Nation of Islam, he had spoken on campuses to audiences that were not predominantly Afro-American. Malcolm's decision to accept the invitation to speak at the Militant Labor Forum, however, was the first time he had agreed to appear on the platform of a meeting outside Harlem or the Black community in any city.

Malcolm told the Young Socialist Alliance leaders who interviewed him a story about a conversation he had had with the Algerian ambassador to Ghana during a trip to Africa in May. The Algerian, Malcolm said, was "a revolutionary in the true sense of the word (and has his credentials as such for having carried on a successful revolution against oppression in his country)."

Malcolm said when he told the Algerian ambassador "that my political, social, and economic philosophy was Black nationalism, he asked me very frankly: Well, where did that leave him? Because he was white. He was an African, but he was Algerian, and to all appearances, he was a white man. . . . So he showed me where I was alienating people who were true revolutionaries dedicated to overturning the system of exploitation that exists on this earth by any means necessary.

"So I had to do a lot of thinking and reappraising of my definition of Black nationalism," Malcolm said. "Can we sum up the solution to the problems confronting our people as Black nationalism? And if you notice, I haven't been using the expression for several months. But I still would be hard pressed to give a specific definition of the overall philosophy which I think is necessary for the liberation of the Black people in this country."

Malcolm X Talks to Young People closes with a tribute to this revolutionary leader by Jack Barnes, one of the young socialists who conducted that interview. The tribute was presented shortly after Malcolm's assassination at a March 1965 memorial meeting hosted by the Militant Labor Forum at its hall in Lower Manhattan. Barnes, who was then national chairman of the Young Socialist Alliance, had met with Malcolm a second time a few days after the January 1965 interview, so Malcolm could approve the final text. An article by Barnes describing the interview and discussions, published in the *Militant* newspaper on the one-year anniversary of Malcolm's death, has been added to this new edition.

＊

Malcolm's December 1964 presentation as part of a debate at Oxford University, which was televised to an audience of millions by the British Broadcasting Corporation, appears in full for the first time ever in this 2002 edition. We would like to thank Jan Carew for supplying a recording of Malcolm's entire presentation; only the concluding portion had previously been available.

The May 1964 speech by Malcolm X at the University of Ghana first appeared in the book *Where To, Black Man? An*

American Negro's African Diary by Ed Smith (Chicago: Quadrangle, 1967). Smith provided additional information about the Ghana trip, as did Alice Windom, who helped schedule Malcolm's activities during his week-long visit there. Among the highlights were his meetings with the country's parliament and Ghanaian president Kwame Nkrumah, as well as a farewell dinner in Malcolm's honor hosted by the Cuban embassy. Alice Windom supplied photographs from the Ghana trip, as well.

❋

"One of the first things I think young people . . . should learn how to do is see for yourself and listen for yourself and think for yourself," Malcolm told the McComb students at the opening of 1965. "Then you can come to an intelligent decision for yourself."

This book shows how hard Malcolm X worked to do just that—to help young people step outside the bourgeois influences that surround them and come to decisions for themselves. What's more, it demonstrates how important an element working with young people was in Malcolm's own decision to commit his life to building an internationalist revolutionary movement in the United States, one that could join in the fight worldwide to wipe racism, exploitation, and oppression off the face of the earth.

Steve Clark
September 2002

STEVE CLARK is the editor of this collection as well as *Malcolm X: February 1965—The Final Speeches*. He is also the editor of *Maurice Bishop Speaks: The Grenada Revolution 1979–83*, and co-author, with Jack Barnes, of "The Politics of Economics: Che Guevara and Marxist Continuity."

ABOUT THE COVER AND ARTIST

The cover portrait of Malcolm X was painted by artist and sculptor Carole Byard. It was part of the six-story Pathfinder Mural in Lower Manhattan that was painted by some eighty volunteer artists from twenty countries. The mural featured portraits of revolutionary and working-class leaders whose speeches and writings are published by Pathfinder, as well as scores of other heroes and heroines of popular revolutionary struggles from 1848 to today. Byard also painted portraits of antislavery fighters Harriet Tubman and Sojourner Truth for the mural.

The Pathfinder Mural was dedicated in 1989 and for seven years attracted visitors, tour groups, and press coverage from across North America and around the world. By 1996 the mural was badly chipped and faded, and the underlying surface was crumbling from the effects of sun, water, and weather. That year, as the wall beneath the mural underwent structural repair, the work was covered over with a protective paneling.

Influenced by her travels in Africa, Carole Byard's paintings, sculpture, and illustrations have won numerous awards. She is the illustrator of more than a dozen children's books and has taught at Parsons School of Design and the Baltimore School for the Arts.

SELVA NEBBIA/PATHFINDER PRESS

The plight of 22 million Afro-Americans in the United States

Malcolm X speaking in Great Hall of the University of Ghana, May 13, 1964.

*"I'm not here to condemn America.
I'm here to tell the truth about the situation of Black
people in America. And if truth condemns America,
then she stands condemned."*

The plight of 22 million
Afro-Americans in the United States

University of Ghana, May 13, 1964

The following talk was presented at the University of Ghana in Legon. The audience, which filled the university's Great Hall, was the largest Malcolm X addressed during his three-week trip to Africa.

The talk was part of a week-long tour in Ghana organized by the Malcolm X Committee, made up of a number of Afro-Americans living in that country. During his visit, Malcolm X gave a press conference, met with Ghanaian president Kwame Nkrumah, and addressed Ghana's parliament and the Kwame Nkrumah Ideological Institute. He spoke with diplomatic personnel from some fifteen countries of Africa, Asia, and Latin America and was honored at several embassy dinners, including a farewell event hosted by the Cuban ambassador, Armando Entralgo.[1]

I intend for my talk to be very informal, because our position in America is an informal position, [*Laughter*] and I find that it is very difficult to use formal terms to describe a very informal position. No condition of any people on earth is more deplorable than the condition, or plight, of the twenty-two million Black people in America. And our condition is so deplorable because we are in a country that professes to be a democracy and professes to be striving to give justice and freedom and equality to everyone who is born under its constitution. If we were born in South Africa or in Angola or some part of this earth where they don't profess to be for freedom,[2] that would be another thing; but when we are born in a country that stands up and represents itself as the leader of the Free World, and you still have to beg and crawl just to get a chance to drink a cup of coffee, then the condition is very deplorable indeed.

So tonight, so that you will understand me and why I speak as I do, it should probably be pointed out at the outset that I am not a politician. I don't know anything about politics. I'm from America but I'm not an American. I didn't go there of my own free choice. [*Applause*] If I were an American there would be no problem, there'd be no need for legislation or civil rights or anything else. So I just try to face the fact as it actually is and come to this meeting as one of the victims of America, one of the victims of Americanism, one of the victims of democracy, one of the victims of a very hypocritical system that is going all over this earth today representing itself as being qualified to tell other people how to run their country when they can't get the dirty things that are going on in their own country straightened out. [*Applause*]

So if someone else from America comes to you to speak, they're probably speaking as Americans, and they speak as people who see America through the eyes of an American. And usually those types of persons refer to America, or that which exists in America, as the American Dream. But for the twenty million of us in America who are of African descent, it is not an American dream; it's an American nightmare. [*Laughter*]

I don't feel that I am a visitor in Ghana or in any part of

Africa. I feel that I am at home. I've been away for four hundred years, [*Laughter*] but not of my own volition, not of my own will. Our people didn't go to America on the *Queen Mary*, we didn't go by Pan American, and we didn't go to America on the *Mayflower*. We went in slave ships, we went in chains. We weren't immigrants to America, we were cargo for purposes of a system that was bent upon making a profit. So this is the category or level of which I speak. I may not speak it in the language many of you would use, but I think you will understand the meaning of my terms.

When I was in Ibadan [in Nigeria] at the University of Ibadan last Friday night, the students there gave me a new name, which I go for—meaning I like it. [*Laughter*] "Omowale," which they say means in Yoruba—if I am pronouncing that correctly, and if I am not pronouncing it correctly it's because I haven't had a chance to pronounce it for four hundred years [*Laughter*]—which means in that dialect, "The child has returned." It was an honor for me to be referred to as a child who had sense enough to return to the land of his forefathers—to his fatherland and to his motherland. Not sent back here by the State Department, [*Laughter*] but come back here of my own free will. [*Applause*]

I am happy and I imagine, since it is the policy that whenever a Black man leaves America and travels in any part of Africa, or Asia, or Latin America and says things contrary to what the American propaganda machine turns out, usually he finds upon his return home that his passport is lifted.[3] Well, if they had not wanted me to say the things I am saying, they should never have given me a passport in the first place. The policy usually is the lifting of the passport. Now I am not here to condemn America, I am not here to make America look bad, but I am here to tell you the truth about the situation that Black people in America find themselves confronted with. And if truth condemns America, then she stands condemned. [*Applause*]

This is the most beautiful continent that I've ever seen; it's the richest continent I've ever seen, and strange as it may seem, I find many white Americans here smiling in the faces of our African brothers like they have been loving them all of the time. [*Laughter and applause*] The fact is, these same whites who in America spit in our faces, the same whites who in America club us brutally, the same whites who in America sic their dogs upon us, just because we want to be free human beings, the same whites who turn their water hoses upon our women and our babies because we want to integrate with them, are over here in Africa smiling in your face trying to integrate with *you*. [*Laughter*]

I had to write a letter back home yesterday and tell some of my friends that if American Negroes want integration, they should come to Africa, because more white people over here—white Americans, that is—look like they are for integration than there is in the entire American country. [*Laughter*] But actually what it is, they want to integrate with the wealth that they know is here—the untapped natural resources which exceed the wealth of any continent on this earth today.

When I was coming from Lagos to Accra Sunday, I was riding on an airplane with a white man who represented some of the interests, you know, that are interested in Africa. And he admitted—at least it was his impression—that our people in Africa didn't know how to measure wealth, that they worship wealth in terms of gold and silver, not in terms of the natural resources that are in the earth, and that as long as the Americans or other imperialists or twentieth-century colonialists could continue to make the Africans measure wealth in terms of gold and silver, they never would have an opportunity to really measure the value of the wealth that is in the soil, and would continue to think that it is *they* who need the Western powers instead of thinking that it is the Western powers who need the people and the continent that is known as Africa. The thing is, I hope I don't mess up anybody's politics or anybody's plots or plans or schemes, but then I think that it can be well proved and backed up.

Ghana is one of the most progressive nations on the African continent primarily because it has one of the most progressive leaders and most progressive presidents. [*Applause*] The president of this nation has done something that no American, no white American, wants to see done—well, I should say "no American" because all the Americans over there are white Americans.

President Nkrumah is doing something there that the government in America does not like to see done, and that is he's restoring the African image. He is making the African proud of the African image; and whenever the African becomes proud of the African image and this positive image is projected abroad, then the Black man in America, who up to now has had nothing but a negative image of Africa—automatically the image that the Black man in America has of his African brothers changes from negative to positive, and the image that the Black man in America has of himself will also change from negative to positive.

And the American racists know that they can rule the African in America, the African-American in America, only as long as we have a negative image of ourselves. So they keep us with a negative image of Africa. And they also know that the day that the image of Africa is changed from negative to positive, automatically the attitude of twenty-two million Africans in America will also change from negative to positive.

And one of the most important efforts to change the image of the African is being made right here in Ghana. And the Ghanaian personality can be picked right out of any group of Africans anywhere on this planet, because you see nothing in him that reflects any kind of feeling of inferiority or anything of that sort. And as long as you have a president who teaches you that you can do anything that anybody else under the sun can do, you got a good man. [*Applause*]

Not only that, we who live in America have learned to measure Black men: the object we use to measure him is the attitude of America toward him. When we find a Black man who's always receiving the praise of the Americans, we become suspicious of him. When we find a Black man who receives honors and all kinds of plaques and beautiful phrases and words from America, we immediately begin to suspect that person. Because it has been our experience that the Americans don't praise any Black man who is really working for the benefit of the Black man, because they realize that when you begin to work in earnest to do things that are good for the people on the African continent, all the good you do for people on the African continent has got to be against someone else, because someone else up to now has benefited from the labor and the wealth of the people on this continent. So our yardstick in measuring these various leaders is to find out what the Americans think about them. And these leaders over here who are receiving the praise and pats on the back from the Americans, you can just flush the toilet and let them go right down the drain. [*Laughter*]

This president here is disliked. Don't think that it's just the American press, it's the government. In America when you find a concerted effort of the press to always speak in a bad way about an African leader, usually that press is actually reflecting government opinion. But America is a very shrewd government. If it knows that its own governmental position will cause a negative reaction from the people that it wants to continue to exploit, it will pretend to have a free press and at the same time sic that free press on a real African leader and stand on the sideline and say that this is not government policy. But everything that happens in America is government policy. [*Laughter*]

Not only is the president of this country disliked, the president of Algeria, Ben Bella, is disliked because he is revolutionary, he's for freedom of everybody. [Egyptian president] Nasser is disliked because he's for freedom of everybody. All of them are referred to as dictators. As soon as they get the mass of their people behind them, they're a dictator. As soon as they have unity of their people in their country, they're a dictator. If there is no division, fighting, and squabbling going on, the leader of that country is a dictator if he is an African; but as long as it is in America, he's just an American president who has the support of the people. [*Laughter and applause*]

I am coming to America in a minute, but I just want to comment on our relations I've noticed since being here. I heard that there is a conflict among some of our brothers and sisters over here concerning whether or not it's advisable for the government to play such a prominent role in guiding the education—the curriculum and whatnot—of the people of the country and in the various universities. Yes, anytime you have a people who have been colonized for as long as our people have been colonized, and you tell them now they can vote, they will spend all night arguing and never get anywhere. Everything needs to be controlled until the colonial mentality has been completely destroyed, and when that colonial mentality has been destroyed at least to the point where they know what they are voting for, then you give them a chance to vote on this and vote on that. But we have this trouble in America, as well as other areas where colonialism has existed, the only way they can practice or apply democratic practices is through advice and counsel.

So my own honest, humble opinion is, anytime you want to come out from under a colonial mentality, let the government set up the educational system and educate you in the direction or way they want you to go in; and then after your understanding is up to the level where it should be, you can stand around and argue or philosophize or something of that sort. [*Laughter and applause*]

There is probably no more enlightened leader on the African continent than President Nkrumah, because he lived in America. He knows what it is like there. He could not live in that land as long as he did and be disillusioned, or confused, or be deceived. Anytime you think that America is the land of the free, you come there and take off your national dress and be mistaken for an American Negro, and you will find out you're not in the land of the free. [*Applause*] America is a colonial power. She is just as much a colonial power in 1964 as France, Britain, Portugal, and all these other European countries were in 1864. She's a twentieth-century colonial power; she's a modern colonial power, and she has colonized twenty-two million African-Americans. While there are only eleven million Africans colonized in South Africa, four or five million colonized in Angola, there are twenty-two million Africans colonized in America right now on May 13, 1964. What is second-class citizenship if nothing but twentieth-century colonialism? They don't want you to know that slavery still exists, so rather than call it slavery they call it second-class citizenship.

Either you are a citizen or you are not a citizen at all. If you are a citizen, you are free; if you are not a citizen, you are a slave. And the American government is afraid to admit that she never gave freedom to the Black man in America and won't even admit that the Black man in America is not free, is not a citizen, and doesn't have his rights. She skillfully camouflages it under these pretty terms of second-class citizenship. It's colonialism, neocolonialism, imperialism . . . [*Inaudible*] [*Laughter*]

One of our brothers just landed here today from New York. He told me that when he left New York, the police were walking in Harlem six abreast. Why? Because Harlem is about to explode. You know what I mean by "Harlem"? Harlem is the most famous city on this earth; there is no city on the African continent with as many Africans as Harlem. In Harlem they call it little Africa, and when you walk through Harlem, you're in Ibadan, everyone there looks just like you. And today the police were out in force, with their clubs. They don't have police dogs in Harlem, 'cause those kind of people who live in Harlem don't allow police dogs to come in Harlem. [*Laughter*] That's the point, they don't allow police dogs to come in Harlem. . . . [*Inaudible*]

They are troubled with the existence of little gangs who have been going around killing people, killing white people.[4] Well now, they project it abroad as an antiwhite gang. No, it's not an antiwhite gang, it's an *antioppression* gang. It's an *antifrustration* gang. They don't know what else to do. They've been waiting for the government to solve their problems; they've been waiting for the president to solve their problems; they've been waiting for the Senate and the Congress and the Supreme Court to solve their problems; they've been waiting for Negro leaders to solve their problems; and all they hear are a lot of pretty words. So they become frustrated and don't know what to do. So they do the only thing they know how: they do the same thing the Americans did when they got frustrated with the British in 1776—liberty or death.

This is what the Americans did; they didn't turn the other cheek to the British. No, they had an old man named Patrick Henry who said, "Liberty or death!" I never heard them refer to him as an advocate of violence; they say he's one of the Founding Fathers, because he had sense to say, "Liberty or death!"

And there is a growing tendency among Black Americans today, who are able to see that they don't have freedom—they are reaching the point now where they are ready to tell the Man no matter what the odds are against them, no matter what the cost is, it's liberty or death. If this is the land of the free, then give us some freedom. If this is the land of justice, then give us some justice. And if this is the land of equality, give us some equality. This is the growing temper of the Black American, of the African-American, of which there are twenty-two million.

Am I justified in talking like this? Let me see. I was in Cleveland, Ohio, just two months ago when this white clergyman was killed by the bulldozer.[5] I was in Cleveland, I was there. Now you know if a white man in the garb, in the outfit, the costume, or whatever you want to call it, of a priest . . . [*Inaudible*] if they run over him with a bulldozer, what will they do to a Black man? They run over someone who looks like them who is demonstrating for freedom, what chance does a Black man have? This wasn't in Mississippi, this was in Cleveland in the North. This is the type of experience the Black man in America is faced with every day. . . . [*Inaudible*]

**Any means necessary
to bring about freedom**

**The oppressed masses
of the world cry out for action
against the common oppressor**

Malcolm X entering hall prior to debate at Oxford University in United Kingdom, December 3, 1964.

"The young generation of whites, Blacks, browns— you're living at a time of extremism, a time of revolution. And I for one will join with anyone I don't care what color you are, as long as you want to change this miserable condition that exists on this earth."

Any means necessary
to bring about freedom

Oxford University, December 3, 1964

The following remarks were given during a program sponsored by the Oxford Union, a student debating society at Oxford University in the United Kingdom. The debate was televised to an audience of millions by the British Broadcasting Corporation. The proposition under debate was "Extremism in defense of liberty is no vice, moderation in the pursuit of justice is no virtue," a statement made by Barry Goldwater in his 1964 speech accepting the Republican Party nomination for president of the United States.

Malcolm X was the fifth of six speakers, and the second of three who defended the above proposition. The other two speaking for it were Eric Abrahams, a student from Jamaica and president of the Oxford Union, and Hugh MacDiarmid, a Scottish poet and member of the Communist Party. Among the three opposing the proposition was Humphrey Berkeley, a Conservative Party member of Parliament, who spoke directly before Malcolm. There was no question period. The audience, which included many students originally from Africa and Asia, greeted Malcolm's remarks with enthusiastic applause. The minutes of the meeting record that in the vote held after the debate, the proposition defended by Malcolm received 137 votes to 288 against.

Mr. Chairman, tonight is the first night that I've ever had an opportunity to be as near to conservatives as I am. [*Laughter*] And the speaker who preceded me—First, I want to thank you for the invitation to come here to the Oxford Union. The speaker who preceded me is one of the best excuses that I know to prove our point concerning the necessity, sometimes, of extremism in the defense of liberty, why it is no vice, and why moderation in the pursuit of justice is no virtue. I don't say that about him personally, but that type is the—[*Laughter and applause*]

He's right. *X* is not my real name. But if you study history, you'll find why no Black man in the Western Hemisphere knows his real name. Some of *his* ancestors kidnapped *our* ancestors from Africa and took us into the Western Hemisphere and sold us there, and our names were stripped from us and so today we don't know who we really are. I'm one of those who admit it, and so I just put *X* up there to keep from wearing his name.

And as far as this apartheid charge that he attributed to me is concerned, evidently he has been misinformed. I don't believe in any form of apartheid. I don't believe in any form of segregation. I don't believe in any form of racialism. But at the same time, I don't endorse a person as being right just because his skin is white. And ofttimes, when you find people like this—I mean that type—[*Laughter*] when a man whom they have been taught is below them has the nerve or firmness to question some of their philosophy or some of their conclusions, usually they put that label on us, a label that is only designed to project an image which the public will find distasteful.

I am a Muslim. If there is something wrong with that, then I stand condemned. My religion is Islam. I believe in Allah. I believe in Muhammad as the apostle of Allah. I believe in brotherhood of all men, but I don't believe in brotherhood with anybody who's not ready to practice brotherhood with our people. [*Applause*] I don't believe in brotherhood—I just take time to make these few things clear, because I find that one of the tricks of the West—and I imagine my good friend, or at least that type [*Laughter*] is from the West—one of the tricks of the West is to use or create images.

They create images of a person who doesn't go along with their views, and they make certain that this image is distasteful, and that anything that that person has to say from there on in is rejected. This is a policy that has been practiced, pretty much, by the West. It perhaps would have been practiced by others had they been in power, but during recent centuries the West has been in power, they've created the images, and they've used these images quite skillfully and quite successfully. That's why today we need a little extremism in order to straighten a very nasty situation out. Or a very extremely nasty situation out. [*Laughter*]

I think the only way one can really determine whether or not extremism in defense of liberty is justified, is not to approach it as an American or a European or an African or an Asian, but as a human being. If we look upon it as different types, immediately we begin to think in terms of extremism being good for one and bad for another, or bad for one and good for another. But if we look upon it, if we look upon ourselves as human beings, I doubt that anyone will deny that extremism in defense of liberty, the liberty of any human being, is no vice. Anytime anyone is enslaved or in any way deprived of his liberty, that person, as a human being, as far as I'm concerned he is justified to resort to whatever methods necessary to bring about his liberty again. [*Applause*]

But most people usually think in terms of extremism as something that's relative, related to someone whom they know or something that they've heard of. I don't think they look upon extremism by itself or all alone. They apply it to something. A good example, and one of the reasons that it can't be too well understood today: many people who have been in positions of power in the past don't realize that the power—centers of power—are changing. When you're in a position of power for a long time, you get used to using your yardstick, and you take it for granted that because you've forced your yardstick upon others, that everyone is still using the same yardstick. So that your definition of extremism usually applies to everyone.

But nowadays times are changing, and the center of power is changing. People in the past who weren't in a position to have a yardstick, or use a yardstick of their own, are using their own yardstick now. And you use one and they use another. In the past, when the oppressor had one stick and the oppressed used that same stick, today the oppressed are sort of shaking the shackles and getting yardsticks of their own. So when they say extremism, they don't mean what you do. And when you say extremism, you don't mean what they do. There's entirely two different meanings. And when this is understood, I think you can better understand why those who are using methods of extremism are being driven to them.

A good example is the Congo.[6] When the people who are in power want to use—again, create an image to justify something that's bad, they use the press, and they'll use the press to create a humanitarian image for a devil, or a devil image for a humanitarian. They'll take a person who's the victim of the crime and make it appear he's the criminal, and they'll take the criminal and make it appear that he's the victim of the crime. And the Congo situation is one of the best examples that I can cite right now to point this out. The Congo situation is a nasty example of how a country, because it is in power, can take its press and make the world accept something that's absolutely criminal.

They take American-trained—they take pilots that they say are American-trained—and this automatically lends respectability to them, [*Laughter*] and then they will call them anti-Castro Cubans. And that's supposed to add to their respectability [*Laughter*] and eliminate the fact that they're dropping bombs on villages where they have no defense whatsoever against such planes, blowing to bits Black women—Congolese women, Congolese children, Congolese babies. This is extremism. But it is never referred to as extremism, because it is endorsed by the West, it's financed by America, it's made respectable by America, and that kind of extremism is never labeled as extremism. Because it's not extremism in defense of liberty. And if it is extremism in defense of liberty, as this talk has just pointed out, it's extremism in defense of liberty for the wrong type of people. [*Applause*]

I'm not advocating that kind of extremism. That's cold-blooded murder. But the press is used to make that cold-blooded murder appear as an act of humanitarianism.

They take it one step farther and get a man named Tshombe, who is a murderer. They refer to him as the premier or the prime minister of the Congo to lend respectability to him. He's actually the murderer of the rightful prime minister of the Congo. [*Applause*] They never mention that this man—I'm not for extremism in defense of that kind of liberty or that kind of activity. They take this man, who's a murderer. The world recognizes him as a murderer. But they make him the prime minister. He becomes a paid murderer, a paid killer, who is propped up by American dollars. And to show the degree to which he is a paid killer, the first thing he does is go to South Africa and hire more killers and bring them into the Congo. They give them the glorious name of mercenary, which means a hired killer; not someone that's killing for some kind of patriotism, or some kind of ideal, but a man who is a paid killer, a hired killer. And one of the leaders of them is right from this country here. And he's glorified as a soldier of fortune, when he's shooting down little Black women and Black babies and Black children.

I'm not for that kind of extremism. I'm for the kind of extremism that those who are being destroyed by those bombs and destroyed by those hired killers are able to put forth to thwart it. They will risk their lives at any cost. They will sacrifice their lives at any cost against that kind of criminal activity.

I'm for the kind of extremism that the freedom fighters in the Stanleyville regime are able to display against these hired killers, who are actually using some of my tax dollars, that I have to pay up in the United States, to finance that operation over there. We're not for that kind of extremism.

And again, I think you must point out that the real criminal there is the—or rather one of the [*Malcolm laughs*]—one of those who are very much involved, as accessories to the crime, is the press. Not so much your press, but the American press, which has tricked your press into repeating what they have invented. [*Laughter and applause*]

But I was reading in one of the English papers this morning, I think it's a paper called the [*Daily*] *Express*. And it gave a very clear account of the type of criminal activity that has been carried on by the mercenaries that are being paid by United States tax dollars. And it showed where they were killing Congolese, whether they were from the central government or the Stanleyville government. It didn't make any difference to them, they just killed them. They had it fixed where those who had been processed had to wear a white bandage around their head. And any Congolese that they saw without that white bandage, they killed him. This is clearly pointed out in the English papers. If they had printed it last week, there would have been an outcry, and no one would have allowed the Belgians and the United States, and the others who are in cahoots with each other, to carry on the criminal activity that they did in the Congo, which I doubt anybody in the world, not even here at Oxford, will accept. Not even my friend. [*Laughter*]

INTERJECTION: Point of [*Inaudible*].

MALCOLM X: Yes?

SAME PERSON: I wonder what—exactly what sort of extremism you would consider killing of missionaries to be? [*From the audience: "Hear, hear!" Applause.*]

MALCOLM X: I'd call it the type of extremism that was involved when America dropped the bomb on Hiroshima and killed 80,000 people, or over 80,000 people, both men, women, children, everything. It was an act of war. I'd call it the same kind of extremism that happened when England dropped bombs on German cities, and Germans dropped bombs on English cities. It was an act of war. And the Congo situation is war. And when you call it war, then anybody that dies, they die a death that is justified. But those who are—[*Protests from audience: "For shame!"*] But those who are in the Stanleyville regime, sir, are defending their country. Those who are coming in, are invading their country, and some of the refugees that were questioned on television in this city a couple days ago pointed out that had the paratroopers not come in, they doubted that they would have been molested. They weren't being molested until the paratroopers came in. [*Applause*]

I don't encourage any acts of murder, nor do I glorify in anybody's death, but I do think that when the white public uses its press to magnify the fact that there are the lives of white hostages at stake—they don't say "hostages," every paper says "white hostages"—they give me the impression that they attach more importance to a white hostage and a white death than they do the death of a human being despite the color of his skin. [*Applause*]

I feel forced to make that point clear, that I'm not for any indiscriminate killing. Nor does the death of so many people go by me without creating some kind of emotion. But I think that white people are making the mistake—and if they read their own newspapers, they will have to agree—that they, in clear-cut language, make a distinction between the type of dying according to the color of the skin. And when you begin to think in terms of death being death, no matter what type of human being it is, then we will all probably be able to sit down as human beings and get rid of this extremism and moderation. But as long as the situation exists as it is, we're going to need some extremism, and I think some of you will need some moderation too.

So why would such an act in the Congo, which is so clearly criminal, be condoned? It's condoned primarily because it has been glorified by the press and has been made to look beautiful, and therefore the world automatically sanctions it. And this is the role that the press plays. If you study back in history, different wars, always the press—Whenever a country that's in power wants to step in, unjustly, and invade someone else's property, they use the press to make it appear that the area that they are about to invade is filled with savages, or filled with people who have gone berserk, or they are raping white women, molesting nuns; they use the same old tactic, year in and year out.

Now there was a time when the dark world, people with dark skin, would believe anything that they saw in the papers that originated in Europe. But today, no matter what is put in the paper, they stop and look at it two or three times and try and figure out what is the motive of the writer. And usually they can determine what the motive of the writer is.

They use the press. The powers that be use the press to give the devil an angelic image and give the image of the devil to the one who's really angelic. They make oppression and exploitation and war actually look like an act of humanitarianism. This is not the kind of extremism that I support, that I go along with.

One of the reasons that I think it's necessary to clarify my own point, personally: I was in a conversation with a student here on the campus yesterday, and she, after we were in a—I think we had coffee or something, dinner. There were several of us. I have to add that in, for those minds of yours that run astray. [*Laughter and applause*]

And she asked me, she told me that, "Well, I'm surprised that you're not what I expected." I said, "What did you mean, what do you mean?" [*Laughter*] She said, "Well, I was looking for your horns." [*Laughter*] And so I told her, "I have them, but I keep them hidden." [*Laughter*] Unless someone draws them out, as my friend, or that type—It takes certain types to draw them out. [*Laughter*]

This is actually true. Usually if a person is looked upon as an extremist, anything that that person does, in your eyesight, is extreme. On the other hand, if a person is looked upon as conservative, just about anything they do is conservative. And this comes again through the manipulating of images. What they want you to think—that a certain area, or a certain person, or a certain group, is extremist, or rather is involved in actions of extremism—the first thing they do is project that person in the image of an extremist. And then anything that he does from then on is extreme, you know, it doesn't make any difference whether it's right or wrong. As far as you're concerned, if the image is wrong, whatever they do is wrong.

And this has been done by the Western press, and also by the American press. And it has been picked up by the English press and the European press. Whenever any Black man in America shows signs of an uncompromising attitude against the injustices that he experiences daily, and shows no tendency whatever to deal or compromise with it, then the American press begins to project that person as a radical and extremist, somebody who's irresponsible, or is a rabble-rouser, or someone who doesn't use—who doesn't rationalize in dealing with the problem.

INTERJECTION: I wonder whether you'd consider that you have seen me projected, rather successfully, a quite unpleasant image of "a type."

MALCOLM X: It depends on which angle—[*Protests from audience*] No, let the gentleman bring out his point. It depends on which angle you look at it, sir. I'm not—I never try and hide what I am. If—

SAME PERSON: I'm referring to more your treatment of the previous speaker.

MALCOLM X: You're referring to my treatment of the previous speaker? [*Laughter and applause*] You make my point, [*Laughter*] that as long as a white man does it, it's all right. A Black man is supposed to have no feelings. [*Applause*] So when a Black man strikes back, he's an extremist. He's supposed to sit passively and have no feelings, be nonviolent, and love his enemy. No matter what kind of attack, be it verbal or otherwise, he's supposed to take it. But if he stands up and in any way tries to defend himself, [*Malcolm laughs*] then he's an extremist. [*Laughter and applause*]

No. I think that the speaker who preceded me is getting exactly what he asked for. [*Laughter*] My reason for believing in extremism—intelligently directed extremism, extremism in defense of liberty, extremism in quest of justice—is because I firmly believe in my heart that the day that the Black man takes an uncompromising step and realizes that he's within his rights, when his own freedom is being jeopardized, to use any means necessary to bring about his freedom or put a halt to that injustice, I don't think he'll be by himself.

I live in America, where there are only 22 million Blacks against probably 160 million whites. One of the reasons that

I'm in no way reluctant or hesitant to do whatever is necessary to see that Black people do something to protect themselves: I honestly believe that the day that they do, many whites will have more respect for them. And there will be more whites on their side than are now on their side with this little wishy-washy "love-thy-enemy" approach that they've been using up to now.

And if I'm wrong, then you are racialists. [*Laughter and applause*]

As I said earlier, in my conclusion, I'm a Muslim. I believe in the religion of Islam. I believe in Allah, I believe in Muhammad, I believe in all of the prophets. I believe in fasting, prayer, charity, and that which is incumbent upon a Muslim to fulfill in order to be a Muslim. In April I was fortunate to make the hajj to Mecca, and went back again in September to try and carry out my religious functions and requirements.

But at the same time that I believe in that religion, I have to point out I'm also an American Negro, and I live in a society whose social system is based upon the castration of the Black man, whose political system is based on castration of the Black man, and whose economy is based upon the castration of the Black man. A society which, in 1964, has more subtle, deceptive, deceitful methods to make the rest of the world think that it's cleaning up its house, while at the same time the same things are happening to us in 1964 that happened in 1954, 1924, and in 1984.

They came up with what they call a civil rights bill in 1964, supposedly to solve our problem, and after the bill was signed, three civil rights workers were murdered in cold blood.[7] And the FBI head, [J. Edgar] Hoover, admits that they know who did it. They've known ever since it happened, and they've done nothing about it. Civil rights bill down the drain. No matter how many bills pass, Black people in that country where I'm from—still, our lives are not worth two cents. And the government has shown its inability, or its unwillingness, to do whatever is necessary to protect life and property where the Black American is concerned.

So my contention is that whenever a people come to the conclusion that the government which they have supported proves itself unwilling or proves itself unable to protect our lives and protect our property because we have the wrong color skin, we are not human beings unless we ourselves band together and do whatever, however, whenever is necessary to see that our lives and our property are protected. And I doubt that any person in here would refuse to do the same thing, were he in the same position. Or I should say, were he in the same condition. [*Applause*]

Just one step farther to see, am I justified in this stand? And I say, I'm speaking as a Black man from America, which is a racist society. No matter how much you hear it talk about democracy, it's as racist as South Africa or as racist as Portugal, or as racist as any other racialist society on this earth. The only difference between it and South Africa: South Africa preaches separation and practices separation; America preaches integration and practices segregation. This is the only difference. They don't practice what they preach, whereas South Africa preaches and practices the same thing. I have more respect for a man who lets me know where he stands, even if he's wrong, than the one who comes up like an angel and is nothing but a devil. [*Applause*]

The system of government that America has consists of committees. There are sixteen senatorial committees that govern the country and twenty congressional committees. Ten of the sixteen senatorial committees are in the hands of southern racialists, senators who are racialists. Thirteen of the twenty—well this was before the last election, I think it's even more so now. Ten of the sixteen committees, senatorial committees, are in the hands of senators who are southern racialists. Thir-

teen of the twenty congressional committees were in the hands
of southern congressmen who are racialists. Which means out
of the thirty-six committees that govern the foreign and domestic direction of that government, twenty-three are in the
hands of southern racialists—men who in no way believe in
the equality of man, and men who'd do anything within their
power to see that the Black man never gets to the same seat or
to the same level that they are on.

The reason that these men from that area have that type of
power is because America has a seniority system. And those
who have that seniority have been there longer than anyone
else because the Black people in the areas where they live can't
vote. And it is only because the Black man is deprived of his
vote that puts these men in positions of power, that gives them
such influence in the government beyond their actual intellectual or political ability, or even beyond the number of
people from the areas that they represent.

So we can see in that country that no matter what the federal government professes to be doing, the power of the federal government lies in these committees. And any time any
kind of legislation is proposed to benefit the Black man or give
the Black man his just due, we find it is locked up in these
committees right here. And when they let something through
the committee, usually it is so chopped up and fixed up that
by the time it becomes law, it's a law that can't be enforced.

Another example is the Supreme Court desegregation decision that was handed down in 1954.[8] This is a law, and they
have not been able to implement this law in New York City, or
in Boston, or in Cleveland, or Chicago, or the northern cities.
And my contention is that any time you have a country, supposedly a democracy, supposedly the land of the free and the
home of the brave, and it can't enforce laws—even in the
northernmost, cosmopolitan, and progressive part of it—that
will benefit a Black man, if those laws can't be enforced or that

law can't be enforced, how much heart do you think we will get when they pass some civil rights legislation which only involves more laws? If they can't enforce this law, they'll never enforce those laws.

So my contention is that we are faced with a racialistic society, a society in which they are deceitful, deceptive, and the only way we can bring about a change is to talk the kind of language—speak the language that they understand. The racialists never understand a peaceful language. The racialist never understands the nonviolent language. The racialist we have, he's spoken his language to us for four hundred years.

We have been the victim of his brutality. We are the ones who face his dogs that tear the flesh from our limbs, only because we want to enforce the Supreme Court decision. We are the ones who have our skulls crushed, not by the Ku Klux Klan but by policemen, only because we want to enforce what they call the Supreme Court decision. We are the ones upon whom water hoses are turned, with pressure so hard that it rips the clothes from our backs—not men, but the clothes from the backs of women and children. You've seen it yourselves. Only because we want to enforce what they call the law.

Well, any time you live in a society supposedly based upon law, and it doesn't enforce its own law because the color of a man's skin happens to be wrong, then I say those people are justified to resort to any means necessary to bring about justice where the government can't give them justice. [*Applause*]

I don't believe in any form of unjustified extremism. But I believe that when a man is exercising extremism, a human being is exercising extremism in defense of liberty for human beings, it's no vice. And when one is moderate in the pursuit of justice for human beings, I say he's a sinner.

And I might add, in my conclusion—In fact, America is one of the best examples, when you read its history, about extremism. Old Patrick Henry said, "Liberty or death!" That's extreme, very extreme. [*Laughter and applause*]

I read once, passingly, about a man named Shakespeare. I only read about him passingly, but I remember one thing he wrote that kind of moved me. He put it in the mouth of Hamlet, I think it was, who said, "To be or not to be"—he was in doubt about something. [*Laughter*] "Whether it was nobler in the mind of man to suffer the slings and arrows of outrageous fortune"—moderation—"or to take up arms against a sea of troubles and by opposing end them."

And I go for that. If you take up arms, you'll end it. But if you sit around and wait for the one who's in power to make up his mind that he should end it, you'll be waiting a long time.

And in my opinion the young generation of whites, Blacks, browns, whatever else there is—you're living at a time of extremism, a time of revolution, a time when there's got to be a change. People in power have misused it, and now there has to be a change and a better world has to be built, and the only way it's going to be built is with extreme methods. And I for one will join in with anyone, I don't care what color you are, as long as you want to change this miserable condition that exists on this earth.

Thank you. [*Applause*]

The day after speaking at London School of Economics in February 1965, Malcolm X traveled to Smethwick, England, in solidarity with the town's Black community. **Above,** Malcolm walks down Marshall Street, where the Smethwick town council had been buying houses as they came up for sale and then refusing to resell them to Blacks or Asians.

"You're trying to make the Black man the victim of every kind of unjust condition imaginable. Then when he explodes, you want him to explode politely! Why, you're dealing with the wrong man at the wrong time in the wrong way."

The oppressed masses
of the world cry out for action
against the common oppressor

London School of Economics, February 11, 1965

The following speech was given at the London School of Economics to a meeting called by the school's Africa Society. No tape recording of the opening section of Malcolm X's remarks has ever been found.

It is only being a Muslim which keeps me from seeing people by the color of their skin. This religion teaches brotherhood, but I have to be a realist—I live in America, a society which does not believe in brotherhood in any sense of the term. Brute force is used by white racists to suppress nonwhites. It is a racist society ruled by segregationists.

We are not for violence in any shape or form, but believe that the people who have violence committed against them should be able to defend themselves. By what they are doing to me they arouse me to violence. People should only be nonviolent as long as they are dealing with a nonviolent person. Intelligence demands the return of violence with violence. Every time you let someone stand on your head and you don't do anything about it, you are not acting with intelligence and should not be on this earth—you won't be on this earth very long either.

I have never said that Negroes should initiate acts of aggression against whites, but where the government fails to protect the Negro he is entitled to do it himself. He is within his rights. I have found the only white elements who do not want this advice given to undefensive Blacks are the racist liberals. They use the press to project us in the image of violence.

There is an element of whites who are nothing but cold, animalistic racists. That element is the one that controls or has strong influence in the power structure. It uses the press skillfully to feed statistics to the public to make it appear that the rate of crime in the Black community, or community of nonwhite people, is at such a high level. It gives the impression or the image that everyone in that community is criminal.

And as soon as the public accepts the fact that the dark-skinned community consists largely of criminals or people who are dirty, then it makes it possible for the power structure to set up a police-state system. Which will make it permissible in the minds of even the well-meaning white public for them to come in and use all kinds of police methods to brutally suppress the struggle on the part of these people against segregation, discrimination, and other acts that are unleashed against them that are absolutely unjust.

They use the press to set up this police state, and they use the press to make the white public accept whatever they do to the dark-skinned public. They do that here in London right now with the constant reference to the West Indian population and the Asian population having a high rate of crime or having a tendency toward dirtiness. They have all kinds of negative characteristics that they project to make the white public draw back, or to make the white public be apathetic when police-state-like methods are used in these areas to suppress the people's honest and just struggle against discrimination and other forms of segregation.

A good example of how they do it in New York: Last summer, when the Blacks were rioting—the riots, actually they weren't riots in the first place; they were reactions against police brutality.[9] And when the Afro-Americans reacted against the brutal measures that were executed against them by the police, the press all over the world projected them as rioters. When the store windows were broken in the Black community, immediately it was made to appear that this was being done not by people who were reacting over civil rights violations, but they gave the impression that these were hoodlums, vagrants, criminals, who wanted nothing other than to get into the stores and take the merchandise.

But this is wrong. In America the Black community in which we live is not owned by us. The landlord is white. The merchant is white. In fact, the entire economy of the Black community in the States is controlled by someone who doesn't even live there. The property that we live in is owned by someone else. The store that we trade with is operated by someone else. And these are the people who suck the economic blood of our community.

And being in a position to suck the economic blood of our community, they control the radio programs that cater to us, they control the newspapers, the advertising, that cater to us. They control our minds. They end up controlling our civic organizations. They end up controlling us economically, politically, socially, mentally, and every other kind of way. They suck our blood like vultures.

And when you see the Blacks react, since the people who do this aren't there, they react against their property. The property is the only thing that's there. And they destroy it. And you get the impression over here that because they are destroying the property where they live, that they are destroying their own property. No. They can't get to the Man, so they get at what he owns. [*Laughter*]

This doesn't say it's intelligent. But whoever heard of a sociological explosion that was done intelligently and politely? And this is what you're trying to make the Black man do. You're trying to drive him into a ghetto and make him the victim of every kind of unjust condition imaginable. Then when he explodes, you want him to explode politely! [*Laughter*] You want him to explode according to somebody's ground rules. Why, you're dealing with the wrong man, and you're dealing with him at the wrong time in the wrong way.

Another example of how this imagery is mastered, at the international level, is the recent situation in the Congo. Here we have an example of planes dropping bombs on defenseless African villages. When a bomb is dropped on an African village, there's no way of defending the people from the bomb. The bomb doesn't make a distinction between men and women. That bomb is dropped on men, women, children, and babies. Now it has not been in any way a disguised fact that planes have been dropping bombs on Congolese villages all during the entire summer. There is no outcry. There is no concern. There is no sympathy. There is no urge on the part of even the so-called progressive element to try and bring a halt to this mass murder. Why?

Because all the press had to do was use that shrewd propaganda word that these villages were in "rebel-held" territory. "Rebel-held," what does that mean? That's an enemy, so anything that they do to those people is all right. You cease to think of the women and the children and the babies in the so-called rebel-held territory as human beings. So that anything that is done to them is done with justification. And the progressives, the liberals don't even make any outcry. They sit twiddling their thumbs, as if they were captivated by this press imagery that has been mastered here in the West also.

They refer to the pilots that are dropping the bombs on these babies as "American-trained, anti-Castro Cuban pilots." As long as they are American-trained, this is supposed to put the stamp of approval on it, because America is your ally. As long as they are anti-Castro Cubans, since Castro is supposed to be a monster and these pilots are against Castro, anybody else they are against is also all right. So the American planes with American bombs being piloted by American-trained pilots, dropping American bombs on Black people, Black babies, Black children, destroying them completely—which is nothing but mass murder—goes absolutely unnoticed. . . . [*Gap in tape*]

They take this man Tshombe—I guess he's a man—and try and make him acceptable to the public by using the press to refer to him as the only one who can unite the Congo. Imagine, a murderer—not an ordinary murderer, a murderer of a prime minister, the murderer of the rightful prime minister of the Congo—and yet they want to force him upon the people of the Congo, through Western manipulation and Western pressures. The United States, the country that I come from, pays his salary. They openly admit that they pay his salary. And in saying this, I don't want you to think that I come here to make an anti-American speech. [*Laughter*] I wouldn't come here for that. I come here to make a speech, to tell you the truth. And if the truth is anti-American, then blame the truth, don't blame me. [*Laughter*]

He's propped up by American dollars. The salaries of the hired killers from South Africa that he uses to kill innocent Congolese are paid by American dollars. Which means that I come from a country that is busily sending the Peace Corps to Nigeria while sending hired killers to the Congo. [*Laughter*] The government is not consistent; something is not right there. And it starts some of my African brothers and sisters that have been so happy to see the Peace Corps landing on their shores to take another look at that thing, and see what it really is.

[*From the audience: "What is it?"*] Exactly what it says: Peace Corps, get a piece of their country. [*Laughter and applause*]

So what the press does with its skillful ability to create this imagery, it uses its pages to whip up this hysteria in the white public. And as soon as the hysteria of the white public reaches the proper degree, they will begin to work on the sympathy of the white public. And once the sympathy reaches the proper degree, then they put forth their program, knowing that they are going to get the support of the gullible white public in whatever they do. And what they are going to do is criminal. And what they are doing is criminal.

How do they do it? If you recall reading in the paper, they never talked about the Congolese who were being slaughtered. But as soon as a few whites, the lives of a few whites were at stake, they began to speak of "white hostages," "white missionaries," "white priests," "white nuns"—as if a white life, one white life, was of such greater value than a Black life, than a thousand Black lives. They showed you their open contempt for the lives of the Blacks, and their deep concern for the lives of the whites. This is the press. And after the press had gotten the whites all whipped up, then anything that the Western powers wanted to do against these defenseless, innocent freedom fighters from the eastern provinces of the Congo, the white public went along with it. [*From the audience: "It's true."*] They know it's true.

So to get towards the end of that, what it has done, just in press manipulation, the Western governments have permitted themselves to get trapped, in a sense, in backing Tshombe, the same as the United States is trapped over there in South Vietnam.[10] If she goes forward she loses, if she backs up she loses. She's getting bogged down in the Congo in the same way.

Because no African troops win victories for Tshombe. They never have. The only war, the only battles won by the African troops, in the African revolution, in the Congo area, were those won by the freedom fighters from the Oriental province. They won battles with spears, stones, twigs. They won battles because their heart was in what they were doing. But Tshombe's men from the central Congo government never won any battles. And it was for this reason that he had to import these white mercenaries, the paid killers, to win some battles for him. Which means that Tshombe's government can only stay in power with white help, with white troops.

Well, there will come a time when he won't be able to recruit any more mercenaries, and the Western powers, who are really behind him, will then have to commit their own troops openly. Which means you will then be bogged down in the Congo the same as you're bogged down over there now in South Vietnam. And you can't win in the Congo. If you can't win in South Vietnam, you know you can't win in the Congo.

Just let me see. You think you can win in South Vietnam? The French were deeply entrenched. The French were deeply entrenched in Vietnam for a hundred years or so. They had the best weapons of warfare, a highly mechanized army, everything that you would need. And the guerrillas come out of the rice paddies with nothing but sneakers on and a rifle [*Laughter*] and a bowl of rice, nothing but gym shoes—tennis shoes—and a rifle and a bowl of rice. And you know what they did in Dien Bien Phu. They ran the French out of there.[11] And if the French were deeply entrenched and couldn't stay there, then how do you think someone else is going to stay there, who is not even there yet. [*From the audience: "You'll have it happen again."*] We'll get to you in a minute. [*Laughter*] I'm going to sit down and you can tell all you want to say. You can even come up here. [*From the audience: "Yes, I was just making the point that it was Chinese—"*] Make it later on. [*Laughter*]

Yes, all of them are brothers. They were still—they had a bowl of rice and a rifle and some shoes. I don't care whether they came from China or South Vietnam. [*The person from the audience continues interrupting; someone else responds,* "*Shut up!*"] And the French aren't there anymore. We don't care how they did it; they're not there anymore. [*Malcolm laughs; laughter from the audience*] The same thing will happen in the Congo.

See, the African revolution must proceed onward, and one of the reasons that the Western powers are fighting so hard and are trying to cloud the issue in the Congo is that it's not a humanitarian project. It's not a feeling or sense of humanity that makes them want to go in and save some hostages, but there are bigger stakes.

They realize not only that the Congo is a source of mineral wealth, minerals that they need. But the Congo is so situated strategically, geographically, that if it falls into the hands of a genuine African government that has the hopes and aspirations of the African people at heart, then it will be possible for the Africans to put their own soldiers right on the border of Angola and wipe the Portuguese out of there overnight.

So that if the Congo falls, Mozambique and Angola must fall. And when they fall, suddenly you have to deal with Ian Smith.[12] He won't be there overnight once you can put some troops on his borders. [*Applause*] Oh yes. Which means it will only be a matter of time before they will be right on the border with South Africa, and then they can talk the type of language that the South Africans understand. And this is the only language that they understand. [*Applause*]

I might point out right here and now—and I say it bluntly—that you have had a generation of Africans who actually have believed that they could negotiate, negotiate, negotiate, and eventually get some kind of independence. But you're getting a new generation that is being born right now, and they are beginning to think with their own mind and see that you can't negotiate upon freedom nowadays. If something is yours by right, then you fight for it or shut up. If you can't fight for it, then forget it. [*Applause*]

So we in the West have a stake in the African revolution. We have a stake for this reason: as long as the African continent was dominated by enemies, and as long as it was dominated by colonial powers, those colonial powers were enemies of the African people. They were enemies to the African continent. They meant the African people no good, they did the African people no good, they did the African continent no good.

And then in the position that they were, they were the ones who created the image of the African continent and the African people. They created that continent and those people in a negative image. And they projected this negative image abroad. They projected an image of Africa in the people abroad that was very hateful, extremely hateful.

And because it was hateful, there are over a hundred million of us of African heritage in the West who looked at that hateful image and didn't want to be identified with it. We shunned it, and not because it was something to be shunned. But we believed the image that had been created of our own homeland by the enemy of our own homeland. And in hating that image we ended up hating ourselves without even realizing it. [*Applause*]

Why? Because once we in the West were made to hate Africa and hate the African, why, the chain-reaction effect was it had to make us end up hating ourselves. You can't hate the roots of the tree without hating the tree, without ending up hating the tree. You can't hate your origin without ending up hating yourself. You can't hate the land, your motherland, the place that you came from, and we can't hate Africa without ending up hating ourselves.

The Black man in the Western Hemisphere—in North America, Central America, South America, and in the Caribbean—is the best example of how one can be made, skillfully, to hate himself that you can find anywhere on this earth.

The reason you're having a problem with the West Indians

right now is because they hate their origin. Because they don't want to accept their origin, they have no origin, they have no identity. They are running around here in search of an identity, and instead of trying to be what they are, they want to be Englishmen. [*Applause*] Which is not their fault, actually. Because in America our people are trying to be Americans, and in the islands you got them trying to be Englishmen, and nothing sounds more obnoxious than to find somebody from Jamaica running around here trying to outdo the Englishman with his Englishness. [*Laughter and applause*]

And I say that this is a very serious problem, because all of it stems from what the Western powers do to the image of the African continent and the African people. By making our people in the Western Hemisphere hate Africa, we ended up hating ourselves. We hated our African characteristics. We hated our African identity. We hated our African features. So much so that you would find those of us in the West who would hate the shape of our nose. We would hate the shape of our lips. We would hate the color of our skin and the texture of our hair. This was a reaction, but we didn't realize that it was a reaction.

Imagine now, somebody got nerve enough, some whites have the audacity to refer to me as a hate teacher. If I'm teaching someone to hate, I teach them to hate the Ku Klux Klan. But here in America, they have taught us to hate ourselves. To hate our skin, hate our hair, hate our features, hate our blood, hate what we are. Why, Uncle Sam is a master hate teacher, so much so that he makes somebody think he's teaching love, when he's teaching hate. When you make a man hate himself, why you really got it and gone. [*Laughter and applause*]

By skillfully making us hate Africa and, in turn, making us hate ourselves, hate our color and our blood, our color became a chain. Our color became to us a chain. It became a prison. It became something that was a shame, something that we felt held us back, kept us trapped.

So because we felt that our color had trapped us, had imprisoned us, had brought us down, we ended up hating the Black skin, which we felt was holding us back. We ended up hating the Black blood, which we felt was holding us back. This is the problem that the Black man in the West has had.

The African hasn't realized that this was the problem. And it was only as long as the African himself was held in bondage by the colonial powers, was kept from projecting any positive image of himself on our continent, something that we could look at proudly and then identify with—it was only as long as the African himself was kept down that we were kept down.

But to the same degree, during these recent years, that the African people have become independent, and they have gotten in a position on that continent to project their own image, their image has shifted from negative to positive. And to the same degree that it has shifted from negative to positive, you'll find that the image of the Black man in the West of himself has also shifted from negative to positive. To the same degree that the African has become uncompromising and militant in knowing what he wants, you will find that the Black man in the West has followed the same line.

Why? Because the same beat, the same heart, the same pulse that moves the Black man on the African continent—despite the fact that four hundred years have separated us from that mother continent, and an ocean of water has separated us from that mother continent—still, the same pulse that beats in the Black man on the African continent today is beating in the heart of the Black man in North America, Central America, South America, and in the Caribbean. Many of them don't know it, but it's true. [*Applause*]

As long as we hated our African blood, our African skin, our Africanness, we ended up feeling inferior, we felt inadequate, and we felt helpless. And because we felt so inferior and so inadequate and so helpless, instead of trying to stand on our own feet and do something for ourselves, we turned to the white man, thinking he was the only one who could do it for us. Because we were taught, we have been taught, that he was the personification of beauty and the personification of success.

At the Bandung Conference in nineteen fifty—[*From the audience: "five"*] five, [*Laughter*] one of the first and best steps toward real independence for nonwhite people took place. The people of Africa and Asia and Latin America were able to get together. They sat down, they realized that they had differences. They agreed not to place any emphasis any longer upon these differences, but to submerge the areas of differences and place emphasis upon areas where they had something in common.[13]

This agreement that was reached at Bandung produced the spirit of Bandung. So that the people who were oppressed, who had no jet planes, no nuclear weapons, no armies, no navies— and despite the fact that they didn't have this, their unity alone was sufficient to enable them, over a period of years, to maneuver and make it possible for other nations in Asia to become independent, and many more nations in Africa to become independent.

And by 1959, many of you will recall how colonialism on the African continent had already begun to collapse. It began to collapse because the spirit of African nationalism had been fanned from a spark to a roaring flame. And it made it impossible for the colonial powers to stay there by force. Formerly, when the Africans were fearful, the colonial powers could come up with a battleship, or threaten to land an army, or something like that, and the oppressed people would submit and go ahead being colonized for a while longer.

But by 1959 all of the fear had left the African continent and the Asian continent. And because this fear was gone, especially in regards to the colonial powers of Europe, it made it impossible for them to continue to stay in there by the same methods that they had employed up to that time.

So it's just like when a person is playing football. If he has the ball and he gets trapped, he doesn't throw the ball away, he passes it to some of his teammates who are in the clear. And in 1959, when France and Britain and Belgium and some of the others saw that they were trapped by the African nationalism on that continent, instead of throwing the ball of colonialism away, they passed it to the only one of their team that was in the clear—and that was Uncle Sam. [*Laughter*] Uncle Sam grabbed the ball [*Laughter and applause*] and has been running with it ever since. [*Laughter and applause*]

The one who picked it up, really, was John F. Kennedy. He was the shrewdest backfield runner that America has produced in a long time—oh yes he was. He was very tricky; he was intelligent; he was an intellectual; he surrounded himself with intellectuals who had a lot of foresight and a lot of cunning. The first thing they did was to give a reanalysis of the problem. They realized they were confronted with a new problem.

The newness of the problem was created by the fact that the Africans had lost all fear. There was no fear in them anymore. Therefore the colonial powers couldn't stay there by force, and America, the new colonial power, neocolonial power, or neoimperialist power, also couldn't stay there by force. So they came up with a "friendly" approach, a new approach which was friendly. Benevolent colonialism or philanthropic imperialism. [*Laughter*] They called it humanitarianism, or dollarism. And whereas the Africans could fight against colonialism, they found it difficult to fight against dollarism, or to condemn dollarism. It was all a token friendship, and all of the so-called benefits that were offered to the African countries were nothing but tokens.

But from '54 to '64 was the era of an emerging Africa, an independent Africa. And the impact of those independent

African nations upon the civil rights struggle in the United States was tremendous. Number one, one of the first things the African revolution produced was rapid growth in a movement called the Black Muslim movement. The militancy that existed on the African continent was one of the main motivating factors in the rapid growth of the group known as the Black Muslim movement, to which I belonged. And the Black Muslim movement was one of the main ingredients in the entire civil rights struggle, although the movement itself never started it. [*Gap in tape*]

They should say thank you for Martin Luther King, because Martin Luther King has held Negroes in check up to recently. But he's losing his grip, he's losing his influence, he's losing his control.

I know you don't want me to say that. But, see, this is why you're in trouble. You want somebody to come and tell you that your house is safe, while you're sitting on a powder keg. [*Laughter and applause*] This is the mentality, this is the level of Western mentality today. Rather than face up to the facts concerning the danger that you're in, you would rather have someone come along and jive you and tell you that everything is all right and pack you to sleep. [*Laughter*] Why, the best thing that anybody can tell you is when they let you know how fed up with disillusionment and frustration the man in your house has become.

So to bring my talk to a conclusion, I must point out that just as John F. Kennedy realized the necessity of a new approach on the African problem—and I must say that it was during his administration that the United States gained so much influence on the African continent. They removed the other colonial powers and stepped in themselves with their benevolent, philanthropic, friendly approach. And they got just as firm a grip on countries on that continent as some of the colonial powers formerly had on that continent. Not only on the African continent but in Asia too. They did it with dollars.

They used a new approach on us in the States, also. Friendly. Whereas formerly they just outright denied us certain rights, they began to use a new, tricky approach. And this approach was to make it appear that they were making moves to solve our problems. They would pass bills, they would come up with Supreme Court decisions. The Supreme Court came up with what they called a desegregation decision in 1954—it hasn't been implemented yet; they can't even implement it in New York City, where I live—outlawing the segregated school system, supposedly to eliminate segregated schooling in Mississippi and Alabama and other places in the South. And they haven't even been able to implement this Supreme Court decision concerning the educational system in New York City and in Boston and some of the so-called liberal cities of the North.

This was all tokenism. They made the world think that they had desegregated the University of Mississippi. This shows you how deceitful they are. They took one Negro, named [James] Meredith, and took all of the world press down to show that they were going to solve the problem [*Laughter*] by putting Meredith in the University of Mississippi. I think it cost them something like $15 million and they had to use about seven thousand troops—one or the other—to put one Black man in the University of Mississippi.

And then *Look* magazine came out with a story afterwards showing the exposé where the attorney general—at that time Robert Kennedy—had made a deal with Governor Barnett. They were going to play a game on the Negro. Barnett was the racist governor from Mississippi. Kennedy was one of these shining liberal progressives—Robert, that is. And they had made a deal, according to *Look* magazine—which all belongs to the same setup, so they must know what they are talking about. [*Laughter and applause*] *Look* magazine said that Robert Kennedy had told Barnett, "Now, since you want the white votes in the South, what you do is you stand in the doorway and pretend like you're going to keep Meredith out. And when I come, I'm going to come with the marshals, and force Meredith in. So you'll keep all the white votes in the South, and I'll get all the Negro votes in the North."[14] [*Laughter and applause*]

This is what we face in that country. And Kennedy is supposed to be a liberal. He's supposed to be a friend of the Negro. He's supposed to be the brother of John F. Kennedy—all of them in the same family. You know, he being the attorney general, he couldn't go down with that kind of deal unless he had the permission of his older brother, who was his older brother at that time.

So they come up only with tokenism. And this tokenism that they give us benefits only a few. A few handpicked Negroes gain from this; a few handpicked Negroes get good jobs; a few handpicked Negroes get good homes or go to a decent school. And then they use these handpicked Negroes, they put 'em on television, blow 'em up, and make it look like you got a whole lot of 'em, when you only got one or two. [*Laughter*]

And this one or two is going to open up his mouth and talk about how the problem is being solved. And the whole world thinks that America's race problem is being solved, when actually the masses of Black people in America are still living in the ghettos and the slums; they still are the victims of inferior housing; they are still the victims of a segregated school system, which gives them inferior education. They are still victims, after they get that inferior education, where they can only get the worst form of jobs.

And they do this very skillfully to keep us trapped. They know that as long as they keep us undereducated, or with an inferior education, it's impossible for us to compete with them for job openings. And as long as we can't compete with them and get a decent job, we're trapped. We are low-wage earners. We have to live in a run-down neighborhood, which means our children go to inferior schools. They get inferior educa-tion. And when they grow up, they fall right into the same cycle again.

This is the American way. This is the American democracy that she tries to sell to the whole world as being that which will solve the problems of other people too. It's the worst form of hypocrisy that has ever been practiced by any government or society anywhere on this earth, since the beginning of time. And if I'm wrong you can—[*Applause*]

It is the African revolution that produced the Black Mus-lim movement. It was the Black Muslim movement that pushed the civil rights movement. And it was the civil rights movement that pushed the liberals out into the open, where today they are exposed as people who have no more concern for the rights of dark-skinned humanity than they do for any other form of humanity.

To bring my talk to a conclusion, all of this created a hot climate, a hot climate. And from 1963, '64 it reached its peak. Nineteen sixty-three was started out in America by all of the politicians talking about this being the hundredth year since the Emancipation Proclamation.[15] They were going to cel-ebrate all over America "a century of progress in race relations." This is the way January and February and March of 1963 started out.

And then Martin Luther King went into Birmingham, Ala-bama, just trying to get a few Negroes to be able to sit down at a lunch counter and drink an integrated cup of coffee. That's all he wanted. [*Laughter and applause*] That's all he wanted. They ended up putting him in jail. They ended up putting thousands of Negroes in jail. And many of you saw on televi-sion, in Birmingham, how the police had these big vicious dogs biting Black people. They were crushing the skulls of Black people. They had water hoses turned on our women, stripping off the clothes from our own women, from our children.

And the world saw this. The world saw what the world had thought was going to be a year which would celebrate a hundred years of progress toward good race relations between white and Black in the United States—they saw one of the most inhuman, savage displays there in that country.

Right after that, this was followed by the assassination of John F. Kennedy, all by the same problem, and Medgar Evers, another one by the same problem. And it ended in the bombing of a church in Alabama where four little girls, Christians, sitting in Sunday school, singing about Jesus, were blown apart by people who claim to be Christians.[16] And this happened in the year 1963, the year that they said in that country would mark a hundred years of good relations between the races.

By 1964—1964 was the year in which three civil rights workers, who were doing nothing other than trying to show Black people in Mississippi how to register and take advantage of their political potential—they were murdered in cold blood. They weren't murdered by some unknown element. They were murdered by an organized group of criminals known as the Ku Klux Klan, which was headed by the sheriff and his deputy and a clergyman. A preacher, a man of the cloth, was responsible for the murder. And when they tell you what was done to the body of that little Black one that they found—all three were murdered, but when they found the three bodies they said that every bone in the body of the Black one was broken, as if these brutes had gone insane while they were beating him to death. This was in 1964.

Now 1965 is here, and you got these same old people, jumping up talking about the "Great Society" now is coming into existence.[17] [Laughter] Nineteen sixty-five will be the longest and the hottest and the bloodiest year that has yet been witnessed in the United States. Why? I'm not saying this to advocate violence. [Laughter] I'm saying this after a careful analysis of the ingredients—the sociological, political dynamite that exists in every Black community in that country.

Africa is emerging. It's making the Black man in the Western Hemisphere militant. It's making him shift from negative to positive in his image of himself and in his confidence in himself. He sees himself as a new man. He's beginning to identify himself with new forces. Whereas in the past he thought of his problem as one of civil rights—which made it a domestic issue, which kept it confined to the jurisdiction of the United States, a jurisdiction in which he could only seek the aid of white liberals within continental United States—today the Black man in the Western Hemisphere, especially in the United States, is beginning to see where his problem is not one of civil rights, but it is rather one of human rights. And that in the human rights context it becomes an international issue. It ceases to be a Negro problem, it ceases to be an American problem. It becomes a human problem, a problem of human rights, a problem of humanity, a problem for the world.

And by shifting his entire position from civil rights to human rights, he puts it on the world stage and makes it possible where today he no more has to rely on only the white liberals within continental United States to be his supporters. But he brings it onto the world stage and makes it possible for all of our African brothers, our Asian brothers, our Latin American brothers, and those people in Europe, some of whom claim to mean right, also to step into the picture and do whatever is necessary to help us to see that our rights are guaranteed us—not sometime in the long future, but almost immediately.

So the basic difference between the struggle of the Black man in the Western Hemisphere today from the past: he has a new sense of identity; he has a new sense of dignity; he has a new sense of urgency. And above all else, he sees now that he has allies. He sees that the brothers on the African continent, who have emerged and gotten independent states, can see that they have an obligation to the lost brother who went astray and then found himself today in a foreign land. They are obligated. They are just as obligated to the brother who's gone away as they are to the brother who's still at home.

And just as you see the oppressed people all over the world today getting together, the Black people in the West are also seeing that they are oppressed. Instead of just calling themselves an oppressed minority in the States, they are part of the oppressed masses of people all over the world today who are crying out for action against the common oppressor.

Thank you. [*Applause*]

**See for yourself,
listen for yourself,
think for yourself**

**Interview with
the 'Young Socialist'**

Above: Protest outside FBI office in New York, June 1965, marking one-year anniversary of murder of civil rights activists Michael Schwerner, James Chaney, and Andrew Goodman in Mississippi. Demonstrators demanded federal protection for civil rights workers in Mississippi and release without bail of some 900 jailed by state authorities. **Inset:** Front page of October 2, 1962, *New York Times*. Headline reports dispatch of federal troops to Mississippi as James Meredith enrolls at University of Mississippi, the first Black ever to do so. Newspaper photos show cops rounding up Black protesters and federal troops detaining Maj. Gen. Edwin Walker for his role in the racist attacks on campus.

"Don't run and try to make friends with somebody who's depriving you of your rights. They're your enemies. Fight them, and you'll get your freedom."

See for yourself, listen for yourself, think for yourself

A discussion with young civil rights fighters from
Mississippi, January 1, 1965

*The following talk was given at the headquarters of the Organi-
zation of Afro-American Unity in the Hotel Theresa in Harlem
to thirty-seven high school-age youth from McComb, Mississippi, who had been involved in civil rights battles there. They had
come to New York City on an eight-day trip sponsored by the Student Nonviolent Coordinating Committee (SNCC). McComb
was where SNCC had begun its voter registration project and organized Mississippi's first sit-in to desegregate public facilities in
1961. During the 1964 voter registration effort racists had bombed
or set afire more than fifteen churches, homes, and businesses in
McComb.*

I was approached, I think we were at the United Nations, and
I met Mrs. Walker, about two or three weeks ago, and she said
that a group of students were coming up from McComb, Mississippi, and wanted to know if I would meet with you and
speak with you. I told her frankly that it would be the greatest
honor that I ever had experienced. Because I have never been

in the state of Mississippi, number one—not through any fault of my own, I don't think—but it's been my great desire to either go there or meet someone from there.

To not take too much of your time, I would like to point out a little incident that I was involved in a short while ago that will give you somewhat of an idea of why I am going to say what I am.

I was flying on a plane from Algiers to Geneva about four weeks ago, with two other Americans. Both of them were white—one was a male, the other was a female. And after we had flown together for about forty minutes, the lady turned to me and asked me—she had looked at my briefcase and saw the initials M and X—and she said, "I would like to ask you a question. What kind of last name could you have that begins with X?"

So I told her, "That's it: X."

She was quiet for a little while. For about ten minutes she was quiet. She hadn't been quiet at all up to then, you know. And then finally she turned and she said, "Well, what's your first name?"

I said, "Malcolm."

She was quiet for about ten more minutes. Then she turned and she said, "Well, you're not *Malcolm X?*" [*Laughter*]

But the reason she asked that question was, she had gotten from the press, and from things that she had heard and read, she was looking for something different, or for someone different.

The reason I take time to tell you this is, one of the first things I think young people, especially nowadays, should learn how to do is see for yourself and listen for yourself and think for yourself. Then you can come to an intelligent decision for yourself. But if you form the habit of going by what you hear others say about someone, or going by what others think about someone, instead of going and searching that thing out for yourself and seeing for yourself, you'll be walking west when you think you're going east, and you'll be walking east when you think you're going west. So this generation, especially of our people, have a burden upon themselves, more so than at any other time in history. The most important thing we can learn how to do today is think for ourselves.

It's good to keep wide-open ears and listen to what everybody else has to say, but when you come to make a decision, you have to weigh all of what you've heard on its own, and place it where it belongs, and then come to a decision for yourself. You'll never regret it. But if you form the habit of taking what someone else says about a thing without checking it out for yourself, you'll find that other people will have you hating your own friends and loving your enemies. This is one of the things that our people are beginning to learn today—that it is very important to think out a situation for yourself. If you don't do it, then you'll always be maneuvered into actually—You'll never fight your enemies, but you will find yourself fighting your own self.

I think our people in this country are the best examples of that. Because many of us want to be nonviolent. We talk very loudly, you know, about being nonviolent. Here in Harlem, where there are probably more Black people concentrated than any place else in the world, some talk that nonviolent talk too. And when they stop talking about how nonviolent they are, we find that they aren't nonviolent with each other. At Harlem Hospital, you can go out here on Friday night, which—today is what, Friday? yes—you can go out here to Harlem Hospital, where there are more Black patients in one hospital than any hospital in the world—because there's a concentration of our people here—and find Black people who claim they're non-violent. But you see them going in there all cut up and shot up and busted up where they got violent with each other.

So my experience has been that in many instances where you

find Negroes always talking about being nonviolent, they're not nonviolent with each other, and they're not loving with each other, or patient with each other, or forgiving with each other. Usually, when they say they're nonviolent, they mean they're nonviolent with somebody else. I think you understand what I mean. They are nonviolent with the enemy. A person can come to your home, and if he's white and he wants to heap some kind of brutality upon you, you're nonviolent. Or he can come put a rope around your neck, you're nonviolent. Or he can come to take your father out and put a rope around his neck, you're nonviolent. But now if another Negro just stomps his foot, you'll rumble with him in a minute. Which shows you there's an inconsistency there.

So I myself would go for nonviolence if it was consistent, if it was intelligent, if everybody was going to be nonviolent, and if we were going to be nonviolent all the time. I'd say, okay, let's get with it, we'll all be nonviolent. But I don't go along—and I'm just telling you how I think—I don't go along with any kind of nonviolence unless everybody's going to be nonviolent. If they make the Ku Klux Klan nonviolent, I'll be nonviolent. If they make the White Citizens' Council nonviolent, I'll be nonviolent.[18] But as long as you've got somebody else not being nonviolent, I don't want anybody coming to me talking any kind of nonviolent talk. I don't think it is fair to tell our people to be nonviolent unless someone is out there making the Klan and the Citizens' Council and these other groups also be nonviolent.

Now I'm not criticizing those here who are nonviolent. I think everybody should do it the way they feel is best, and I congratulate anybody who can be nonviolent in the face of all that kind of action that I read about in that part of the world. But I don't think that in 1965 you will find the upcoming generation of our people, especially those who have been doing some thinking, who will go along with any form of nonviolence unless nonviolence is going to be practiced all the way around.

If the leaders of the nonviolent movement can go into the white community and teach nonviolence, good. I'd go along with that. But as long as I see them teaching nonviolence only in the Black community, then we can't go along with that. We believe in equality, and equality means you have to put the same thing over here that you put over there. And if just Black people alone are going to be the ones who are nonviolent, then it's not fair. We throw ourselves off guard. In fact, we disarm ourselves and make ourselves defenseless.

Now to try and give you a better understanding of our own position, I guess you have to know something about the Black Muslim movement, which is supposed to be a religious movement in this country, which was extremely militant, vocally militant, or militantly vocal. The Black Muslim movement was supposed to be a religious group. And because it was supposed to be a religious group, it never involved itself in civic matters, so it claimed. And by not getting involved in civic matters, what it did, being militant, it attracted the most militant Negroes, or Afro-Americans, in this country, which it actually did. The Black Muslim movement attracted the most dissatisfied, impatient, and militant Black people in this country.

But when it attracted them, the movement itself, by never involving itself in the real struggle that's confronting Black people in this country, in a sense has gotten maneuvered into a sort of a political and civic vacuum. It was militant, it was vocal, but it never got into the battle itself.

And though it professed to be a religious group, the people from the part of the world whose religion it had adopted didn't recognize them or accept them as a religious group. So it was also in a religious vacuum. It was in a vacuum religiously, by claiming to be a religious group and by having adopted a religion which actually rejected them or wouldn't accept them.

So religiously it was in a vacuum. The federal government tried to classify it as a political group, in order to maneuver it into a position where they could label it as seditious, so that they could crush it because they were afraid of its uncompromising, militant characteristics. So for that reason, though it was labeled a political group and never took part in politics, it was in a political vacuum. So the group, the Black Muslim movement itself, actually developed into a sort of a hybrid, a religious hybrid, a political hybrid, a hybrid-type organization.

Getting all of these very militant Black people into it, and then not having a program that would enable them to take an active part in the struggle, it created a lot of dissatisfaction among its members. It polarized into two different factions—one faction that was militantly vocal, and another faction that wanted some action, militant action, uncompromising action. Finally the dissatisfaction developed into a division, the division developed into a split, and many of its members left. Those who left formed what was known as the Muslim Mosque, Inc., which is authentically a religious organization that is affiliated with and recognized by all of the official religious heads in the Muslim world. This was called the Muslim Mosque, Inc., whose offices are here.

But this group, being Afro-American or being Black American, realized that although we were practicing the religion of Islam, still there was a problem confronting our people in this country that had nothing to do with religion and went above and beyond religion. A religious organization couldn't attack that problem according to the magnitude of the problem, the complexity of the problem itself. So those in that group, after analyzing the problem, saw the need, or the necessity, of forming another group that had nothing to do with religion whatsoever. And that group is what's named and is today known as the Organization of Afro-American Unity.

The Organization of Afro-American Unity is a nonreligious

group of Black people in this country who believe that the problems confronting our people in this country need to be reanalyzed and a new approach devised toward trying to get a solution. Studying the problem, we recall that prior to 1939 in this country, all of our people—in the North, South, East, and West, no matter how much education we had—were segregated. We were segregated in the North just as much as we were segregated in the South. And even right now, today, there's as much segregation in the North as there is in the South. There's some worse segregation right here in New York City than there is in McComb, Mississippi; but up here they're subtle and tricky and deceitful, and they make you think that you've got it made when you haven't even begun to make it yet.

Prior to 1939 our people were in a very menial position or condition. Most of us were waiters and porters and bellhops and janitors and waitresses and things of that sort. It was not until war was declared in Germany by Hitler, and America became involved in a manpower shortage in regards to her factories plus her army—it was only then that the Black man in this country was permitted to make a few strides forward. It was never out of some kind of moral enlightenment or moral awareness on the part of Uncle Sam. Uncle Sam only let the Black man take a step forward when he himself had his back to the wall.

In Michigan, where I was brought up at that time, I recall that the best jobs in the city for Blacks were waiters out at the country club. And in those days if you had a job waiting table in the country club, you had it made. Or if you had a job at the State House. Having a job at the State House didn't mean that you were a clerk or something of that sort—you had the shoeshine stand in the State House. Just by being in there where you could be around all these big politicians, that made you a big-shot Negro. You were shining shoes, but you were a big-shot Negro because you were around big-shot white people and you could bend their ear and get up next to them. And ofttimes in those days, you were chosen to be the voice of the Negro community.

Also right at this time, 1939 or '40, '41, they weren't drafting Negroes in the army or the navy. A Negro couldn't join the navy in 1940 or '41 in this country. He couldn't join. They wouldn't take a Black man in the navy. They would take him if they wanted and make him a cook. But he couldn't just go and join the navy. And he couldn't just go—I don't think he could just go and join the army. They weren't drafting him when the war first started.

This is what they thought of you and me in those days. For one thing, they didn't trust us. They feared that if they put us in the army and trained us on how to use rifles and other things, that we might shoot at some targets that they hadn't picked out. And we would have. Any thinking man knows what target to shoot at. And if a man doesn't, if he has to have someone else to choose his target, then he's not thinking for himself—they're doing the thinking for him.

So it was only when the Negro leaders—they had the same type of Negro leaders in those days that we have today—when the Negro leaders saw all the white fellows being drafted and taken into the army and dying on the battlefield, and no Negroes were dying because they weren't being drafted, the Negro leaders came up and said, "We've got to die too. We want to be drafted too, and we demand that you take us in there and let us die for our country too." This is what the Negro leaders said, back in 1940, I remember. A. Philip Randolph was one of the leading Negroes in those days who said it, and he's one of the Big Six right now; and this is why he's one of the Big Six right now.[19]

They started drafting Negro soldiers then, and then they started letting Negroes get into the navy—but not until Hitler and Tojo[20] and the foreign powers were strong enough to bring pressure upon this country, so that it had its back to the wall and it needed us. At that same time, they let us work in factories. Up until that time we couldn't work in the factories. I'm talking about the North as well as the South. And when they let us work in the factories we began—at first when they let us in we could only be janitors. Then, after a year or so passed by, they let us work on machines. We became machinists, got a little skill. And as we got a little more skill, we made a little more money, which enabled us to live in a little better neighborhood. When we lived in a little better neighborhood, we went to a little better school, got a little better education, and could come out and get a little better job. So the cycle was broken somewhat.

But the cycle was not broken because of some kind of sense of moral responsibility on the part of the government. No, the only time that cycle was broken even to a degree was when world pressure was brought to bear upon the United States government and they were forced to look at the Negro—and then they didn't even look at us as human beings, they just put us into their system and let us advance a little bit farther because it served their interests. But they never let us advance a little bit farther because they were interested in our interests, or interested in us as human beings. Any of you who have a knowledge of history, sociology, political science, or the economic development of this country and its race relations, all you have to do is take what I'm telling you and go back and do some research on it and you'll have to admit that this is true.

It was during the time that Hitler and Tojo were able to make war with this country and put pressure upon them that Negroes in this country advanced a little bit. At the end of the war with Germany and Japan, then Joe Stalin and Communist Russia were a threat. And during that period we made a little bit more advances.

Now the point that I'm making is this: Never at any time in

the history of our people in this country have we made advances or advancement, or made progress in any way just based upon the internal good will of this country, or based upon the internal activity of this country. We have only made advancement in this country when this country was under pressure from forces above and beyond its control. Because the internal moral consciousness of this country is bankrupt. It hasn't existed since they first brought us over here and made slaves out of us. They trick up on the confirmation and make it appear that they have our good interests at heart. But when you study it, every time, no matter how many steps they take us forward, it's like we're standing on a—what do you call that thing?—a treadmill. The treadmill is moving backwards faster than we're able to go forward in this direction. We're not even standing still—we're walking forward, at the same time we're going backward.

I say that because the Organization of Afro-American Unity, in studying the process of this so-called progress during the past twenty years, realized that the only time the Black man in this country is given any kind of recognition, or shown any kind of favor at all, or even his voice is listened to, is when America is afraid of outside pressure, or when she's afraid of her image abroad. We could see that as long as we sat around and carried on our struggle at a level or in a manner that involved only the good will of the internal forces of this country, we would continue to go backward, there would be no real meaningful changes made. So the Organization of Afro-American Unity saw that it was necessary to expand the problem and the struggle of the Black man in this country until it went above and beyond the jurisdiction of the United States.

For the past fifteen years the struggle of the Black man in this country was labeled as a civil rights struggle, and as such it remained completely within the jurisdiction of the United States. You and I could get no kind of benefits whatsoever other than that which would be forthcoming from Washington, D.C. Which meant, in order for it to be forthcoming from Washington, D.C., all of the congressmen and the senators would have to agree to it.

But the most powerful congressmen and the most powerful senators were from the South. And they were from the South because they had seniority in Washington, D.C. And they had seniority because our people in the South, where they came from, couldn't vote. They didn't have the right to vote.

So when we saw that we were up against a hopeless battle internally, we saw the necessity of getting allies at the world level or from abroad, from all over the world. And so immediately we realized that as long as the struggle was a civil rights struggle, was under the jurisdiction of the United States, we would have no real allies or real support. We decided that the only way to make the problem rise to the level where we could get world support was to take it away from the civil rights label, and put in the human rights label.

It is not an accident that the struggle of the Black man in this country for the past ten or fifteen years has been called a struggle for civil rights. Because as long as you're struggling for civil rights, what you are doing is asking these racist segregationists who control Washington, D.C.—and they control Washington, D.C., they control the federal government through these committees—as long as this thing is a civil rights struggle, you are asking it at a level where your so-called benefactor is actually someone from the worst part of this country. You can only go forward to the degree that they let you.

But when you get involved in a struggle for human rights, it's completely out of the jurisdiction of the United States government. You take it to the United Nations. And any problem that is taken to the United Nations, the United States has no say-so on it whatsoever. Because in the UN she only has one vote, and in the UN the largest bloc of votes is African; the continent of Africa has the largest bloc of votes of any continent on this earth. And the continent of Africa, coupled with the Asian bloc and the Arab bloc, comprises over two-thirds of the UN forces, and they're the dark nations. That's the only court that you can go to today and get your own people, the people who look like you, on your side—the United Nations.

This could have been done fifteen years ago. It could have been done nineteen years ago. But they tricked us. They got ahold of our leaders and used our leaders to lead us right back to their courts, knowing that they control their courts. So the leaders look like they're leading us against an enemy, but when you analyze the struggle that we've been involved in for the past fifteen years, the good or the progress that we've made is actually disgraceful. We should be ashamed to even use the word "progress" in the context of our struggle.

So there has been a move on—and I will conclude in a moment—there has been a move on to keep the Negro thinking in this country that he was making strides in the civil rights field, only for the purpose of distracting him and not letting him know that were he to acquaint himself with the structure of the United Nations and the politics of the United Nations, the aim and the purpose of the United Nations, he could lift his problem into that world body. And he'd have the strongest stick in the world that he could use against the racists in Mississippi.

But one of the arguments against getting you and me to do this has always been that our problem is a domestic problem of the United States. And as such, we should not think to put it at a level where somebody else can come and mess with United States domestic affairs. But you're giving Uncle Sam a break. Uncle Sam's got his hands in the Congo, in Cuba, in South America, in Saigon. Uncle Sam has got his bloody hands in every continent and in everybody else's business on this earth. But at the same time, when it comes to taking forceful action in this country where our rights are concerned, he's always going to tell you and me, "Well, these are states' rights." Or he'll make some kind of off-the-wall alibi that's not a bona fide alibi—not because it's an alibi, but to justify his inactivity where your and my rights are concerned.

We were successful when we realized that we had to bring this to the United Nations. We knew that we had to get support, we had to get world support, and that the most logical part of the world to look in for support is among people who look just like you and me.

I was fortunate to be able to take a tour of the African continent during the summer—the Middle East and Africa. I went to Egypt, then to Arabia, Kuwait, Lebanon, and then to Sudan, Ethiopia, Kenya, Tanganyika, Zanzibar, Nigeria, Ghana, Guinea, Liberia, and Algeria. I found while I was traveling on the African continent—I had already detected it in May—that someone has very shrewdly planted the seeds of division on this continent to make the Africans not show genuine concern with our problem, just as they plant seeds in your and my minds so that we won't show concern with the African problem. They try and make you and me think that we're separate, and the two problems are separate.

When I went back this time and traveled to those different countries, I was fortunate enough to spend an hour and a half with Nasser in Egypt, which is a North African country; and three hours with President Nyerere in Tanganyika, which has now become Tanzania, which is an East African country; and with Prime Minister Obote, Milton Obote, in Uganda, which is also an East African country; and with Jomo Kenyatta in Kenya, which is another East African country; and with President Azikiwe in Nigeria, President Nkrumah in Ghana, and President Sékou Touré in Guinea.

I found that in every one of these African countries, the head of state is genuinely concerned with the problem of the Black man in this country, but many of them thought that if they opened their mouths and voiced concern, that they would be insulted by the American Negro leaders. Because one head of state in Asia voiced his support of the civil rights struggle and a couple of the Big Six had the audacity to slap his face and say they weren't interested in that kind of help—which in my opinion is asinine.[21] So that the African leaders only had to be convinced that if they took an open stand at the governmental level and showed interest in the problem of Black people in this country, that they wouldn't be rebuffed.

And today you'll find in the United Nations—and it's not an accident—that every time the Congo question or anything on the African continent is being debated in the Security Council, they couple it with what's going on, or what is happening to you and me, in Mississippi and Alabama and these other places. In my opinion, the greatest accomplishment that was made in the struggle of the Black man in America in 1964 toward some kind of real progress was the successful linking together of our problem with the African problem, or making our problem a world problem. Because now, whenever anything happens to you in Mississippi, it's not a case of just somebody in Alabama getting indignant, or somebody in New York getting indignant. Whatever happens in Mississippi today, with the attention of the African nations drawn toward Mississippi at a governmental level, then the same repercussions that you see all over the world when an imperialist or foreign power interferes in some section of Africa, you see repercussions, you see the embassies being bombed and burned and overturned. Nowadays, when something happens to Black people in Mississippi, you will see the same repercussions all over the world.

I wanted to point this out to you, because it is important for you to know that when you're in Mississippi you're not alone. But as long as you think you're alone, then you take a stand as if you're a minority or as if you're outnumbered, and that kind of stand will never enable you to win a battle. You've got to know that you've got as much power on your side as that Ku Klux Klan has on its side. And when you know that you've got just as much power on your side as the Klan has on its side, you'll talk the same kind of language with that Klan as that Klan is talking with you.

I'll say one more thing, and then I'll conclude.

When I say the same kind of language, I should explain what I mean. See, you can never get good relations with anybody that you can't communicate with. You can never have good relations with anybody that doesn't understand you. There has to be an understanding. Understanding is brought about through dialogue. Dialogue is communication of ideas. This can only be done in a language, a common language. You can never talk French to somebody who speaks only German and think you're communicating. Neither of them—they don't get the point. You have to be able to speak a man's language in order to make him get the point.

Now, you've lived in Mississippi long enough to know what the language of the Ku Klux Klan is. They only know one language. If you come up with another language, you don't communicate. You've got to be able to speak the same language they speak, whether you're in Mississippi, New York City, or Alabama, or California, or anywhere else. When you develop or mature to the point where you can speak another man's language on his level, that man gets the point. That's the only time he gets the point. You can't talk peace to a person who doesn't know what peace means. You can't talk love to a person who doesn't know what love means. And you can't talk any form of nonviolence to a person who doesn't believe in nonviolence. Why, you're wasting your time.

So I think in 1965—whether you like it, or I like it, or we like it, or they like it, or not—you will see that there is a generation of Black people born in this country who become mature to the point where they feel that they have no more business being asked to take a peaceful approach than anybody else takes, unless everybody's going to take a peaceful approach.

So we here in the Organization of Afro-American Unity, we're with the struggle in Mississippi 1,000 percent. We're with the efforts to register our people in Mississippi to vote 1,000 percent. But we do not go along with anybody telling us to help nonviolently. We think if the government says that Negroes have a right to vote, and then when Negroes go out to vote some kind of Ku Klux Klan is going to put them in the river, and the government doesn't do anything about it, it's time for us to organize and band together and equip ourselves and qualify ourselves to protect ourselves. [*Applause*] And once you can protect yourself, you don't have to worry about being hurt. That's it. [*Applause*]

Discussion period

So we're going to have a few minutes now for you to ask questions on all that that has been said, and all that that hasn't been said.

Yes, sir.

QUESTIONER: Could you please say something on the Freedom Democratic Party?

MALCOLM X: Yes. We support the Freedom Democratic Party. We have a statement that we're making in support. We had a rally last Sunday night—no, a week ago Sunday night, to which we invited Mrs. Hamer. She spoke and explained the position of the Mississippi Freedom Democratic Party, and we support it.[22] We know that in Washington—

To give you an example of why we support this, it has as much effect on New York City as it does in Mississippi.

But by the same token, I must point out that those who are depriving you of your rights in Mississippi aren't all in Mississippi. You got these New York Democrats who are just as much responsible. The mayor of this city is a Democrat. The senator, you've heard of him, Robert Kennedy, he's a Democrat. The president of the country is a Democrat. The vice president is a Democrat. Now don't you tell me anything about a Democrat in Mississippi who is depriving you of your rights, when the power of the Democratic Party is in Washington, D.C., and in New York City, and in Chicago, and some of these northern cities.

When you put the power or the pressure upon these people who walk around here posing as liberals—

In New York City Negroes can already vote. When you make known in the city of New York the position of the Mississippi Freedom Democratic Party, and why it was necessary to form that party, and what that party is trying to do toward ousting these illegal representatives from Mississippi, then the Negroes in New York City know what it's all about. We want to know, where does [Mayor Robert] Wagner stand, since he's one of the most powerful and influential leaders of the Democratic Party in the United States. And we want to know where the senator, Robert Kennedy, stands, since he's also one of the most powerful and influential leaders of the Democratic Party in the United States. And we've got a Negro [J. Raymond Jones] who's the assistant to the mayor in this city. We want to know where he stands. Plus you got Lyndon B. Johnson and Hubert Humphrey, who professes to drool at the mouth over Negroes, to let you know where they stand before January 4.[23]

When you get that kind of action off some of these northern Democrats, then you'll get some action in Mississippi. You don't have to worry about that man in Mississippi. The power of the Democratic Party are these people up here who hold all the power in the North.

So we're with you, but we want to go all the way.

See, as a Muslim, I don't get my religion involved in my politics, because they clash. They don't clash, but when you go into something as a Muslim, you've got a whole lot of Negroes who are Christians, who aren't broad-minded enough, so you get into a religious argument, and it doesn't pay.

So I don't enter into this struggle as a Muslim, inasmuch as I enter into it as a member of the Organization of Afro-American Unity. And the stand that the Organization of Afro-American Unity takes is that we get into it without compromising.

You compromise when you're wrong. You don't have to compromise when you're right. Why, you're right. They're not giving you something. This is yours. If you were born in this country, nobody's doing you any favor when they let you vote or when they let you register. They're only recognizing you as a human being and recognizing your right as a human being to exercise your right as a citizen. So they're not doing you any favors.

As long as you approach this thing like somebody has done you a favor, or that you're dealing with a friend, you never can fight that fight. Because when they deal with you, they're not dealing with you like they're dealing with a friend. They look at you like you're an enemy. Now you have to look at them just as if they're an enemy. And once you know what it is you're dealing with, you can deal with that thing. But you can't deal with them with love. Why, man, if there was any love with them, if there was any love in them, you wouldn't have any fight in Mississippi. There's no love there. You have to realize that there's no love there, and then you don't be looking for it, and go ahead and fight them.

When you go to vote or register and someone gets in your way, you're supposed to answer them in the same way that they answer you. When you answer them that way, you get a little dialogue. And if you don't have enough of them down there to do it, we'll come down there and help you do it. Because we are tired of this old runaround that our people have been given in this country.

For a long time they accused me of not getting involved in politics. They should've been glad I didn't get involved in politics, because anything I get in, I'm in it all the way. Now if they say that we don't take part in the Mississippi struggle, we will organize brothers here in New York who know how to handle these kinds of affairs, and they'll slip into Mississippi like Jesus slipped into Jerusalem. [*Laughter and applause*]

This doesn't mean that we're against white people, but we sure are against the Ku Klux Klan and the White Citizens' Councils. Anything that looks like it's against us, we're against it.

Excuse me for raising my voice, but this thing, you know, it gets me upset. Even being involved in a discussion in a country that's supposed to be a democracy. Imagine that, in a country that's supposed to be a democracy, supposed to be for freedom and all of that kind of stuff that they tell you when they want to draft you and put you in the army and send you to Saigon to fight for them. And then you've got to turn around and all night long discuss how you're going to just get a right to register and vote without being murdered. Why, that's the most hypocritical governmental half-truth that has ever been invented since the world was the world.

Yes, ma'am.

QUESTIONER: The question I have is what does the Afro-American Unity do?

MALCOLM X: First, Afro-American means us.

QUESTIONER: I know what it means, I just want to know: What does it do?

MALCOLM X: How do you mean?

QUESTIONER: What kind of struggles, what does it do?

MALCOLM X: Well, first, it was patterned after the OAU. The

OAU is the Organization of African Unity. And the reason we patterned our organization after theirs was they had trouble on the African continent similar to ours. Meaning that there were many independent countries that were so divided against each other that they couldn't come together in a united effort and resolve any of their problems. So some of the more mature African politicians were able to work behind the scenes and get a common understanding, out of which materialized the Organization of African Unity, the purpose of which was to get all African leaders to see the necessity of de-emphasizing their areas of disagreement and emphasizing their areas of agreement, where they had common interests.

This led to the Organization of African Unity being formed, and today they work together in unity and harmony, although there are diverse philosophies, diverse personalities. All of these differences exist; still they can unite together for a common objective.

So studying their problems, and seeing that their problems were similar to ours, we formed ours after the letter and spirit of that OAU, only with an O-A-*A*-U.[24]

Our first objective is—our first step was to find an area of agreement among Afro-Americans. We found that you have the nationalists, you have the civil rights groups, you have all these diverse elements in the Black community. Some want separation, some want integration; some want this, some want that. So how are you going to find something that they all agree upon? You won't find the nationalists agree on civil rights, because they think it's a farce. You won't find the nationalists agree on integration, because they think it's a farce. They haven't seen anyplace where it has ever materialized. It's only a word, something that's played around, kicked around.

So we had to find something that both the nationalists and the integrationists would agree upon. And we found that all of them would agree on the necessity of our people in this country being respected and recognized as human beings. So instead of launching our struggle at the civil rights level that would cause a whole lot of argument, we launched it at the human rights level. And we know that anybody that's for civil rights has got to be for human rights, whether you're an integrationist or a separationist or what you are; you still have to be for human rights.

So our first platform was that we recognized the right of the Black man in the Western Hemisphere to exercise his rights as a human being. Rights that he was born with, rights that no government has the power to give him. God makes you a human being, and God is the one who gives you your human rights, not a government, or some senators, or a judge, or some representatives. And so this is our stand. We are human beings, and our fight is to see that every Black man, woman, and child in this country is respected and recognized as a human being.

Our method is: any means necessary. That's our motto. We're not restricted to this, or confined to that. We reserve the right to use any means necessary to protect our humanity, or to make the world see that they respect us as human beings. Any means necessary.

When I say that, I don't mean anything illegal. The government—You're being treated criminally. The criminal is the one who's illegal. The one who's responsible for these criminal conditions, he's a criminal, he's illegal. And whatever you've got to do to stop this crime from being committed against you, as far as I'm concerned you're not illegal.

So that's our first step at the international level. And politically, we devise and support any program that's designed to give the Black man in this country an opportunity to participate as a citizen, a free citizen, in this political system and in this society. We will involve ourselves in programs of our own, or in anyone else's programs, as long as it doesn't involve any kind of compromise in its approach to getting our people in this country the rights to register and to vote in whichever direction they desire to.

QUESTIONER: [*Inaudible*]

MALCOLM X: The voter registration?

SAME QUESTIONER: How do you support voter registration?

MALCOLM X: We ourselves have our own voter registration drive in the areas where we are, plus we work with other civil rights groups who also have voter registration drives.

SAME QUESTIONER: Do you run candidates?

MALCOLM X: No. Not as yet. . . . [*Inaudible*] What's the word? We keep it to ourselves. We keep it confidential. We will never let you know how many members we have.

SAME QUESTIONER: I'm not asking that.

MALCOLM X: I learned that. I'm giving you some light without you asking. That's one thing I learned in the Black Muslim movement that I found most important: never let anybody know what they're dealing with—its size, its strength, its nothing. The reason for that is, I found, if you're in the jungle or in the woods and you hear something rustling in the bush, you don't know what kind of gun to reach for until you know what's making that noise. Because you might pull out a rabbit gun for an elephant, or you might pull out an elephant gun for a rabbit, and you look foolish either way. It's not good to ever let too much of what you are come out above the ground. The most important part of the tree is the roots, and the roots always remain beneath the ground. That's where the tree gets its life. And the tree dies only when you put those roots up where the light is and it dries up.

So our membership—its nature, its caliber, its content, all of that—we keep it to ourselves. But you see here and there, wherever you find dissatisfied Negroes, if they're not our blood brothers, they're at least some relatives, some relation. If we're not blood brothers, we're at least related.

Any more?

QUESTIONER: We obviously can't say—

MALCOLM X: You from Mississippi too?

SAME QUESTIONER: No, I'm not.

MALCOLM X: I didn't think so. [*Laughter*] Keep on asking.

SAME QUESTIONER: Obviously you can't say what you do. I just was wondering what kind of—

MALCOLM X: It's not a case of I can't say what we do. I told you that we involve ourselves in our own programs to get our people registered, as registered voters in this area and wherever else we are. And we work with any other group that's trying to get our people registered so that they can vote. This is in this political area or in the area of politics. Now what else did you want to know, since you don't seem to be satisfied?

SAME QUESTIONER: Well, maybe. Some others . . . [*Inaudible*]

ANOTHER QUESTIONER: Do you think—

MALCOLM X [*to first questioner*]: No, if that's not clear, ask me. I mean, if I didn't clarify your question, go ahead and dig into it a little deeper.

FIRST QUESTIONER: No, I think that lady from the other group of people—

SECOND QUESTIONER: . . . [*Inaudible*] who can vote, don't vote either, which makes it look like—

MALCOLM X: This is true, which shows you that the reluctance on the part of the Negro to vote isn't always because they don't have the right to. The political history of our people in this country has been that usually you have political machines in most states and in most cities. And they select, as a rule, not Black people to run in the Black community who are intellectually capable to deal with politics as it is, but puppets that serve as their mouthpiece to control the politics of the community. The Black people in Harlem have witnessed this thing year in and year out and have seen how the politics of Harlem and other Negro communities have been pretty much controlled from outside.

So it's not that they're politically lethargic or dead, but they purposely have abstained. But when you give them something to point toward, or vote for, you'll find that they'll be just as active as they've been inactive.

It's the purpose of the OAAU to work among that element of inactive Black people, who have been politically inactive in this area. We intend to charge them and get them active out here, so that we can get a little action. Because those are the real activists. Those who haven't been involved in politics actively are the ones who get involved in physical action. They have not seen anything that could be made to materialize through politics in the past, so they didn't resort to politics. They resorted to things physical, to methods physical, if you understand what I mean.

What we intend to do is try and harness their energy by giving them an understanding of politics, first. Because we don't think that anybody should get us registered as voters and not at the same time give us some education in regards to politics. We don't think that a voter registration program on its own is sufficient. But in line with any voter registration program among Negroes, there must be a voter education program to make our people enlightened in regards to the science of politics, so that they will know what politics is supposed to produce and what the politician is supposed to produce, what his responsibilities are. And then we can't be exploited.

But if you just get Negroes out here and register them, then what you're going to have are more Negroes whose political energy can be exploited by the big city political machines. We don't think that that will ever solve our problems. There has to be voter education as well as voter registration. Most of the Negro politicians don't want this, because those who have been politicians haven't really been trying to solve our problems, inasmuch as they've been getting the handouts from the machine for keeping us in check. When the people realize that, the people wake up.

One of the reasons, if I may add, that Negroes haven't been actively involved in politics is, when the Negro leader—when Negroes go out to try and make other Negroes get registered to vote, they have the wrong motives, usually—especially the politicians. The young students who are doing it today are a little different. But the politician, when he tries to get you registered to vote, he's not interested in making you enlightened so you can vote. He wants you to stay in the dark but register. Then maybe you'll vote for him, or vote for his party, or vote for what he's got going for him. He's not even interested in your condition. And this is why you find Negroes in Harlem haven't gotten involved.

But don't think that they can't get involved. You can get as many Negroes interested politically in Harlem overnight, but you've got to give him something, give him something that he will see will materialize. And I think that our people in this area are ready.

QUESTIONER: [*Inaudible*]

MALCOLM X: Well, there wouldn't have to be necessarily any particular party to make them have something to look forward to, especially up around here. It takes something else to make these people in Harlem feel that they have something to look forward to.

QUESTIONER: [*Inaudible*]

MALCOLM X: No, not particularly. Although, the only real power in this government is politics—and money. The only thing that people recognize is power and money. Power—that's all they recognize. That's why I say, in Mississippi you can love all you want. They don't recognize love, they recognize power. Power. You can love, look how long you've been loving, that's proof of it. You've been loving them like a blind—

QUESTIONER: It's not love—

MALCOLM X: Yeah, I understand, but—[*Laughter*]

SAME QUESTIONER: Don't let love . . . [*Inaudible*]

MALCOLM X: Brother, I will read the breakdown, you know, in Mississippi—in various counties. Many of the counties, now, you got more Negroes than you got whites. Negroes outnumber the whites. And you see, freedom comes only two ways. There's only two ways that a person gets freedom: either by the ballot or by bullets.

QUESTIONER: [*Inaudible*] the riot you had here?

MALCOLM X: In Harlem?

SAME QUESTIONER: Yes.

MALCOLM X: It wasn't a riot. That was a pogrom. You know what a pogrom is? How do you say that? Pogrom. Pogrom is what it was. Pogrom. That wasn't any riot, that was a pogrom. That was the police heaping brutality upon the people of the area. It was a setup.

SAME QUESTIONER: All right, the way I understood it, though, the police brutalized [*Inaudible*] . . . The riot was protesting against police brutality. I heard it when I got to New York. Could I ask you, what was actually accomplished by this so-called riot?

MALCOLM X: It wasn't a riot. There was a rumor passed on to us in May that the police in New York during the summer were going to try and provoke trouble, so that they could step in and crush the organizing and growth of militant groups that they were afraid, if they were allowed to grow, would get to the size that they could never be controlled.

If you study the characteristics of that so-called riot, every action on the part of the police in Harlem was designed to draw out groups that they felt were equipped and ready to do this thing. The tactics that the police used were designed to draw fire back. They were firing guns at people who didn't have guns. But they were firing to get somebody to fight, to shoot back. The police know you got just as many guns in Harlem as there are in Saigon right now. But none of the groups in Harlem that were equipped and qualified to strike back got involved. None of them got involved.

But the whole thing was set up to try and get them involved, so that they could be crushed while they were still in their embryonic, so-called embryonic stage. As you said, it goes beyond the Mississippi situation. But all of our problems are the same: wrong color.

QUESTIONER: [*Inaudible*]

MALCOLM X: Whether it was the COFO?[25]

SAME QUESTIONER: Right.

MALCOLM X: Any program that's designed to get our people registered is good, especially in Mississippi. Because our people in Mississippi outnumber—there's a greater percentage of our people in the state of Mississippi than there is, probably, in any other state. If the people in Mississippi did have voting rights, what's his name—[Sen. James] Eastland—wouldn't be in Washington, D.C. None of those powerful senators and congressmen who control the committees in Washington, D.C., would be there.

So any effort on the part of any group that gets our people in the state of Mississippi registered, that's good. But my only criticism is sending people on the front lines against well-armed enemies and telling them: Don't fight. Why, that's insane. I can't go along with that. No.

When those three brothers were murdered down there, it was a drag, it's been a drag on the part of the civil rights groups, the way they've just taken that thing so easy. Hardly nothing has happened. They're telling everybody to be patient, be loving and long-suffering when the whole world is on your side. If you went on the rampage in Mississippi, wouldn't nobody hold it against you. Because the whole world knows that the people down there are the worst things on this earth.

So we go for the operation, but we don't go for sending anybody to a front line and telling them, don't protect themselves. No. Then, after one of your soldiers gets killed, every-body says, well, you're supposed to keep on loving anyway? No, I can't go along with that.

That's what split the Muslim movement. That's what caused the Black Muslim movement to be split. Some of our broth-ers got hurt and nothing was done about it. Those of us who wanted to do something about it were kept from doing some-thing about it. So we split.[26]

No, I don't go along with any kind of action that ties up my hands and then put me in the ring with Sonny Liston or Cassius Clay. [*Laughter*] No, don't tie my hands, unless you're going to tie up their hands too. Then it's fair.

You don't see the white man sending his people to war some-where and tying up their hands. No, and if those two hadn't been white, you wouldn't even have known that that happened in Mississippi, because they kill Negroes in Mississippi every day. Ever since we've been here.

I was over in Africa, brother, while all that was going on. And I read about it and I know that it tore the Africans up. Tore 'em up. Why, if you had thrown bombs right and left in Mis-sissippi, you'd have had the world on your side.

I'm not telling you to throw bombs. I'm just telling you what would happen. [*Laughter*] If I told you that, if somebody started throwing bombs around here tomorrow, they'd blame me, put the blame on me. They would never give me credit, but they'd put the blame on me.

Only from Mississippi. Questions. Are you from Mississip-pi? Are there any other questions?

I hope that you don't think that I'm trying to incite you. But look here, just look at yourselves. Some of you all are teenag-ers, students. Now how do you think I feel—and I belong to a generation ahead of you—how do you think I feel having to tell you, "We, my generation, sat around like a knot on the wall while the whole world was actually fighting for what were its

"Young people all over the world are the ones who are actually involving themselves in the struggle to eliminate oppression and exploitation."

Above: With students at Tuskegee Institute in Alabama, where Malcolm X addressed several thousand students, February 3, 1965.
Bottom: Malcolm X with U.S. volunteers at high school in Tanzania for exiled members of liberation organizations from countries across Southern Africa, October 1964.

"Anytime you live in a society that doesn't enforce its own law because the color of a man's skin happens to be wrong, then I say those people are justified to resort to any means necessary to bring about justice."

Above: youth stand their ground before Alabama cop during "Battle of Birmingham," May 1963.

Facing page, top: Malcolm X participating in protest in Los Angeles against cop killing of Nation of Islam member Ronald Stokes, May 1963. **Middle:** three young people in New York City run from police during second day of rebellion against cop killings in Harlem, summer 1964. **Bottom:** over 400,000 students in New York City boycott segregated school system, February 3, 1964.

"You can't separate the militancy that's displayed on the African continent from the militancy displayed right here among American Blacks."

Above: 1960 protest in South Africa against racist Pass Laws, internal passports required of all nonwhites, Johannesburg City Hall. **Facing page top:** supporters welcome Ahmed Ben Bella upon arrival in Algiers, 1962. Ben Bella became president of popular revolutionary government in Algeria established after seven-year war of national liberation defeated French colonial power. **Middle:** December 3, 1960: Congolese prime minister Patrice Lumumba (on right) and comrades the day after capture by pro-imperialist forces. **Bottom:** protest against U.S.-Belgian intervention in Congo held at United Nations in New York, December 4, 1964. Third from left is Clifton DeBerry, Socialist Workers Party 1964 presidential candidate, at whose initiative this and similar actions were called nationwide.

"Young people are living at a time of revolution, a time when there's got to be a change."

Above: Malcolm X and Fidel Castro at Hotel Theresa in Harlem during Castro's trip to New York to address UN General Assembly, September 1960. **Facing page top:** demonstration by Vietnamese youth. Banner reads, "Chi Lang village youth volunteer in anti-U.S. war of national salvation." Sign at left says, "Nothing is more precious than independence and freedom." **Middle:** march against Vietnam War in San Francisco, April 15, 1967. Protesters carry banner, "The NLF 'Viet Cong' Never Called Us Nigger". **Bottom:** during October 1962 "missile" crisis, Cuban Militia members find a moment to relax and entertain fellow fighters.

"You have to wake the people up first, to their humanity, to their own worth. Then you'll get action."

Above: protest in Cincinnati, April 12, 2001, against police killing of Timothy Thomas, a 19-year-old Black youth. **Bottom:** Palestinian youth hurl rocks at armored vehicle of Israeli occupation forces, Gaza Strip, September 2001.

VAL LIBBY/MILITANT

ADEL HANA/ASSOCIATED PRESS

human rights"—and you've got to be born into a society where you still have that same fight. What did we do, who preceded you? I'll tell what we did: nothing. And don't you make the same mistake we made.

You tell me why a Black man in this society has to wait on the Supreme Court and a white man doesn't have to wait on the Supreme Court. Yet both of them are men.

You tell me why the Congress and the Senate have got to make a Black man a human being, and the same Congress and Senate don't have to make a white man a human being, if they're both men.

You tell why you need a presidential proclamation to get respect and recognition, and a white man doesn't need it, if we're both men.

I'll tell you why: we're not both men.

A man will die and fight for what is his right. And if he doesn't, if he's not ready to fight and die for what is his right, he's not a man. That's the only way you can look at it. And when you begin to look like you're going to . . . [*Inaudible*] you get what belongs to a man.

But as long as you sit around here waiting on some court that is headed by a Ku Klux Klan judge, or waiting on a Senate that's controlled by a Ku Klux Klan senator, or a Congress that's controlled by a White Citizens' Council congressman, or a White House that's got just as much Klan influence in it as any other part of the country, why, no, you'll never be respected as a human being.

I must say this: I was in Africa, I was in Kenya. Five years ago, one of the men in Africa who had the worst image was Kenyatta. They tried to make you and me think that Kenyatta, Jomo Kenyatta, was a monster. I met Kenyatta. I flew from Tanganyika to Zanzibar to Kenya with Kenyatta, and everybody respects him. He's known now as the father of the country. The white man respects him and the Black man respects him. Five years ago they said he was a leader of the Mau Mau.[27] And they tried to make him appear to be a monster. As long as he didn't have his own independence, he was a monster.

But today Kenyatta is so highly respected it's not an accident that when the brothers in Stanleyville had all these hostages in the Congo, and they wanted to try and save them, who did they choose to moderate the conference that took place between Ambassador Atwood and Tom Kanza in Nairobi? Jomo Kenyatta. The same man that this government and this society was labeling as a monster five years ago, now they turn to him when statesmanship is needed. He had a negative image five years ago because he wouldn't compromise. He was bringing freedom to his people by any means necessary. Now that his people have gotten their freedom, he's respected.

And this is the only way you'll get it. You get freedom by not being confined. You get freedom by letting your enemy know that you'll do anything to get your freedom. You'll get it. It's the only way you'll get it. Then, when you get that kind of attitude, they'll label you as a "crazy Negro," or they'll call you a "crazy nigger"—they don't say Negro. They say, "That nigger's crazy." Or they'll call you an extremist or they'll call you a subversive, or seditious, or a Red, or a radical. But when you stay radical long enough, and get enough people to be just like you, you'll get your freedom. Then, after you get your freedom, they'll talk about what a great person you are, just like they do with Kenyatta. So if Lumumba had lived long enough and consolidated the Congo, they'd talk about him like a great person, because he'd be free and independent.

So don't you run around here trying to make friends with somebody who's depriving you of your rights. They're not your friends. No, they're your enemies. Treat them like that and fight them, and you'll get your freedom. And after you get your freedom, your enemy will respect you. [*Applause*] He *will* respect you.

I say that with no hate. I have no hate in me. I have no hate at all. I don't have any hate. But I've got some sense. [*Laughter*] I think I've got some sense. I'm not going to let somebody who hates me tell me to love him. I'm not that way-out. And you, young as you are, and because you start thinking, you're not going to do it either. The only time you're going to get in that kind of bag is if somebody puts you in there, somebody else, who doesn't have your welfare at heart.

[*Inaudible comment from audience*]

[*Malcolm laughs*] Ah yes, I'm going to explain it. I'm just going to take five more minutes, because Sharon Jackson reminded me of something which I think is very important. It's why at the beginning I mentioned, when I was on this plane, how I rode right next to this man and woman for an hour, and they didn't have the slightest idea who I was, because they were looking for somebody with horns. Usually white people think anybody who is not going to be cool and calm under their extreme brutality has got horns. So this is done by image making. People who make images use images to make you hate their enemies and love your own. No: hate their friends and love their enemies. They use images to do this.

One place they've done it is in the Congo. The Congo is where they told me and you we came from. All my life, when I was a little boy, they said we came out of Africa, and they made believe we came out of the Congo, because that was supposed to be the most savage part of Africa. So you know, we're probably more closely related to the brothers in the Congo than anybody else. And when you hear them talking about cannibals, they're talking about our cousins, about our brothers, you know. If you really want to believe it. But they aren't any more cannibalistic in the Congo than they are in the downtown, there in the Village. There's some real cannibals down there in the Village. [*Laughter*] They'll be eating up anything, you know. [*Laughter*]

In this country what they try and make it appear is that the people in the Congo are savages. And they do this very skillfully in order to justify their being over there. Now when I was in Tanganyika, Dar es Salaam—I think it was in October—some American Negroes, Afro-Americans who live in Dar es Salaam, came to me and told me about this Congolese who was cussing them out. And I asked them, why . . . [*Gap in tape*]

. . . African village. Now you know a village has no air force. A village has no defense against bombs that are being dropped on it. And the pilot in the plane can't tell who the bomb is being dropped upon. It's just being dropped on a village.

So here you have American airplanes being flown by what they call "anti-Castro Cuban, American-trained pilots." Now you see how slick they are. The reason they say "American-trained pilots" is to make you automatically side with them, because they are American-trained. The reason they say they are anti-Castro Cuban pilots is because Castro's already a monster, and if somebody links these people, that they're against Castro, then whoever else they're against, it's all right. It's what you call a journalistic, psychological trick on your mind.

So now you have airplanes that are dropping bombs on Black women, Black children, and Black babies, blowing them to bits in the Congo. They justify it by making it appear to be a humanitarian project. And they get big Negroes in this country to talk to you and tell you that America is justified in doing it. You show me a big Negro and usually he's their big Negro. And his job is to make you and me think that no matter how much atrocity they are committing, that they are right. And they do it with these tricks.

How can you justify dropping a bomb on a village—not a civilization that has all the weapons of warfare, but a village? You don't need to drop a bomb on a village that doesn't even have rifles in it. But it shows you their complete lack of concern for life when that life is clothed in a black skin.

To show you again how merciless they are. They take Tshombe. Tshombe is a Black man, but he's a murderer. He murdered this man called Patrice Lumumba, in cold blood. And this government took Tshombe away from Spain.[28] And this government did do it, because I know people who can tell you how certain high members of this country's State Department got on board a plane with a certain African leader and flew all the way almost to his country, trying to get this African leader to use his influence on other African leaders to make Tshombe acceptable to the people of the African continent. And this happened almost a year before they brought Tshombe back down—to show you what a plot, what a conspiracy that they're involved in.

And here Tshombe is a killer, a murderer—of Patrice Lumumba. They put him over the government in Léopoldville, and then they used the press to give him an image of acceptability by saying he's the only one that can restore peace to the Congo. Imagine this, he's a murderer. It's like saying Jesse James is the only one can run the bank. Therefore you should let Jesse James run the bank; and the only reason the bank is in trouble is because Jesse James already was in the bank. [*Laughter*]

So just to go one step farther. They take Tshombe and give him enough money to go to South Africa and bring white mercenaries, hired killers, in to fight for him. A mercenary is someone who kills for pay. He doesn't kill because he's patriotic. He doesn't kill because he's loyal. He kills anything in sight for pay, and this is what America is using your tax dollars to support: a Black murderer who hires white murderers to shoot down his own people. Because America knows if she went in and did it, the world wouldn't go along with her.

And then, when these white murderers are heaping so much butchery upon the people in the Oriental province of the Congo, the brothers in the Oriental province are forced to start using some of the methods to keep these white mercenaries and white hired killers from wiping them out. So they shoot hostages. The only reason they held hostages was to keep America's mercenaries from dropping bombs on them. It's the only thing they could do. They held the hostages not because they were cannibals. And they didn't eat people like they're trying to say in the newspapers. Why would they wait to this late date to eat some white meat, when they been over there all those years? And they went in there at a time when they were probably more tasty than they are in times like this.

At the time the hostages were being held, the American government—rather the Congolese government from Stanleyville—sent an emissary, Tom Kanza, their foreign minister, to Kenya, and he was negotiating with Atwood, the ambassador to Kenya from America, at a meeting which Kenyatta was mediating. And at the time that this was going on, it was then that America dropped the paratroopers in Stanleyville. At no time did the Africans or the Congolese in any way harm any white hostages until those paratroopers were dropped. And I think it's America that harmed more than one. If they were savages, there wouldn't have been a white hostage seen. How are you going to come out of the sky and save some hostages that are already in my hands, when I've got some machine guns? No. If you save some, it means that I'm human and I treated them in a humane way, because I didn't wipe them all out when I see your airplane coming.

So this old stuff you hear about the government trying to make you think that their being in the Congo is something humanitarian—it's the most criminal operation that has ever been carried on by a so-called civilized government since history was recorded!

The United States was the one responsible there. And you will find that she will suffer over there, because the only way she can hold Tshombe in power is to send in more white troops. The Black troops don't fight for Tshombe. He needs white troops. And there are too many Black troops fighting against those white troops for them to win, for the white ones to win, which means more whites will have to be added to it and added to it and added to it.

And first thing you know they'll be hung up in the same kind of situation that they got themselves bogged down in South Vietnam right now. Because all the African nations combined will fight there in the Congo. You don't need a whole lot of heavy war machinery to fight a war nowadays. All you need is some darkness and a little lighting equipment. [*Laughter*] That equalizes things.

We got about three more minutes. Three more minutes.

Well, I want to thank all of you for taking the time to come to Harlem and especially here. I hope that you have gotten a better understanding of us. I put it to you just as plain as I know how to put it; there's no interpretation necessary. And I want you to know that we're not in any way trying to advocate any kind of indiscriminate, unintelligent action. But we will go along with you in any kind of intelligent action that you are involved in to protect the lives and property of our people in this country. Any kind of action that you're ever involved in that's designed to protect the lives and the property of our mistreated people in this country, we're with you 1,000 percent. And if you don't feel that you are qualified to do it, we have some brothers who will slip in, as I said earlier, and help train you and show you how to equip yourself in such a manner to deal with these people who need to be dealt with.

And before you dismiss, let me see one of those. . . . [*Inaudible*] I would like to read you this—it's brief—before you leave. It says:

"We applaud the efforts of James Farmer and the other civil rights groups to block the seating of the five illegal representatives from Mississippi when Congress convenes on January 4. We are pleased to see that Mr. Farmer and his civil rights colleagues are so dead earnest in backing the election challenges that have been initiated by the Mississippi Freedom Democratic Party. As chairman of the Organization of Afro-American Unity, I want to state emphatically that we support all uncompromising efforts made by all well-meaning people to unseat the illegal representatives from the state of Mississippi and any other area where our people are denied the right to vote simply because they have been born with dark skin.

"We also insist that since over 97 percent of the Black Americans supported Lyndon B. Johnson, Hubert Humphrey, Robert Kennedy, and the Democratic Party in the recent elections, which is the most overwhelming support given by any minority group to one party and its candidates, I am challenging Lyndon B. Johnson, Hubert Humphrey, and Robert Kennedy, to declare exactly where they stand on the seating of these illegal representatives from Mississippi before January 4."

And they *should* state their case.

"We applaud the lead that has been taken by New York representative William Fitts Ryan in blocking the seating of these Mississippi congressmen, and the firm stand taken at his side by Adam Clayton Powell.[29] Since Mayor Wagner will be in Harlem later this year to obtain the political support of our people in order to remain in City Hall, I challenge Mayor Wagner and his chief assistant, J. Jones, also to let nearly one and a half million Black Americans in New York City know where they stand on the plan to seat illegal representatives before January 4.

"I, for one, along with some friends, plan to be in Washington on January 4 as an observer. We wish to witness and record the stand taken by the so-called liberals, who are seekers of our people's political support at poll time, for we plan to be 100 percent active in all political areas from 1965 onward." [*Applause*]

So I thank you and I hope to see you in Mississippi myself in January.[30] Thank you. [*Applause*]

Malcolm X talks to staff members of the Tuskegee Institute *Campus Digest* in Tuskegee, Alabama, February 3, 1965.

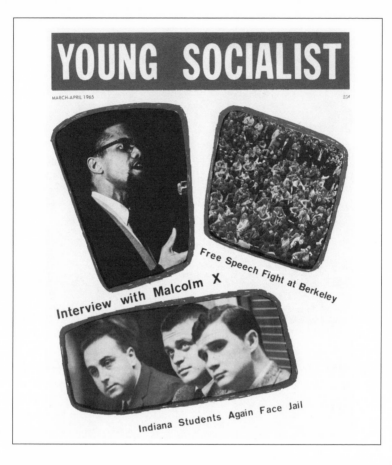

The March-April 1965 *Young Socialist* featuring the interview with Malcolm X also contained articles about the free speech fight taking place at the University of California at Berkeley around attempts by the campus administration to prevent students from soliciting funds to support the civil rights movement, as well as an international campaign to defend three members of the Young Socialist Alliance at Indiana University indicted in May 1963 on charges of advocating the overthrow of the government of the United States and State of Indiana.

"I'm reaching out to true revolutionaries dedicated to overturning the system of exploitation that exists on this earth by any means necessary."

Interview with the 'Young Socialist'

Hotel Theresa, Harlem, January 18, 1965

Malcolm X gave the following interview in January 1965 to Jack Barnes, national chairman of the Young Socialist Alliance, and Barry Sheppard, a staff writer for the Militant *newspaper. Both Sheppard and Barnes were members of the editorial board of the* Young Socialist *magazine. At a later meeting with Barnes, Malcolm went over and approved the final text, which then appeared in the March-April 1965 issue of the* Young Socialist.

YOUNG SOCIALIST: What image of you has been projected by the press?

MALCOLM X: Well, the press has purposely and skillfully projected me in the image of a racist, a race supremacist, and an extremist.

YOUNG SOCIALIST: What's wrong with this image? What do you really stand for?

MALCOLM X: First, I'm not a racist. I'm against every form of racism and segregation, every form of discrimination. I believe in human beings, and that all human beings should be respected as such, regardless of their color.

YOUNG SOCIALIST: Why did you break with the Black Muslims?

MALCOLM X: I didn't break, there was a split. The split came about primarily because they put me out, and they put me out because of my uncompromising approach to problems I thought should be solved and the movement could solve.

I felt the movement was dragging its feet in many areas. It didn't involve itself in the civil or civic or political struggles our people were confronted by. All it did was stress the importance of moral reformation—don't drink, don't smoke, don't permit fornication and adultery. When I found that the hierarchy itself wasn't practicing what it preached, it was clear that this part of its program was bankrupt.[31]

So the only way it could function and be meaningful in the community was to take part in the political and economic facets of the Negro struggle. And the organization wouldn't do that because the stand it would have to take would have been too militant, uncompromising, and activist, and the hierarchy had gotten conservative. It was motivated mainly by protecting its own self-interests.

I might also point out that although the Black Muslim movement professed to be a religious group, the religion they had adopted—Islam—didn't recognize them. So religiously it was in a vacuum. And it didn't take part in politics, so it was not a political group. When you have an organization that's neither political nor religious and doesn't take part in the civil rights struggle, what can it call itself? It's in a vacuum. So all of these factors led to my splitting from the organization.

YOUNG SOCIALIST: What are the aims of your new organization?

MALCOLM X: There are two organizations. There's the Muslim Mosque, Inc., which is religious. Its aim is to create an atmosphere and facilities in which people who are interested in

Islam can get a better understanding of Islam. The aim of the other organization, the Organization of Afro-American Unity, is to use whatever means necessary to bring about a society in which the twenty-two million Afro-Americans are recognized and respected as human beings.

YOUNG SOCIALIST: How do you define Black nationalism, with which you have been identified?

MALCOLM X: I used to define Black nationalism as the idea that the Black man should control the economy of his community, the politics of his community, and so forth.

But when I was in Africa in May, in Ghana, I was speaking with the Algerian ambassador who is extremely militant and is a revolutionary in the true sense of the word (and has his credentials as such for having carried on a successful revolution against oppression in his country). When I told him that my political, social, and economic philosophy was Black nationalism, he asked me very frankly: Well, where did that leave him? Because he was white. He was an African, but he was Algerian, and to all appearances, he was a white man. And he said if I define my objective as the victory of Black nationalism, where does that leave him? Where does that leave revolutionaries in Morocco, Egypt, Iraq, Mauritania? So he showed me where I was alienating people who were true revolutionaries dedicated to overturning the system of exploitation that exists on this earth by any means necessary.

So I had to do a lot of thinking and reappraising of my definition of Black nationalism. Can we sum up the solution to the problems confronting our people as Black nationalism? And if you notice, I haven't been using the expression for several months. But I still would be hard pressed to give a specific definition of the overall philosophy which I think is necessary for the liberation of the Black people in this country.

YOUNG SOCIALIST: Is it true, as is often said, that you favor violence?

MALCOLM X: I don't favor violence. If we could bring about recognition and respect of our people by peaceful means, well and good. Everybody would like to reach his objectives peacefully. But I'm also a realist. The only people in this country who are asked to be nonviolent are Black people. I've never heard anybody go to the Ku Klux Klan and teach them nonviolence, or to the [John] Birch Society and other right-wing elements. Nonviolence is only preached to Black Americans, and I don't go along with anyone who wants to teach our people nonviolence until someone at the same time is teaching our enemy to be nonviolent. I believe we should protect ourselves by any means necessary when we are attacked by racists.

YOUNG SOCIALIST: What do you think is responsible for race prejudice in the U.S.?

MALCOLM X: Ignorance and greed. And a skillfully designed program of miseducation that goes right along with the American system of exploitation and oppression.

If the entire American population were properly educated—by properly educated, I mean given a true picture of the history and contributions of the Black man—I think many whites would be less racist in their feelings. They would have more respect for the Black man as a human being. Knowing what the Black man's contributions to science and civilization have been in the past, the white man's feelings of superiority would be at least partially negated. Also, the feeling of inferiority that the Black man has would be replaced by a balanced knowledge of himself. He'd feel more like a human being. He'd function more like a human being, in a society of human beings.

So it takes education to eliminate it. And just because you have colleges and universities doesn't mean you have education. The colleges and universities in the American educational system are skillfully used to miseducate.

YOUNG SOCIALIST: What were the highlights of your trip to Africa?

MALCOLM X: I visited Egypt, Arabia, Kuwait, Lebanon, Sudan, Ethiopia, Kenya, Tanganyika, Zanzibar (now Tanzania), Nigeria, Ghana, Liberia, Guinea, and Algeria. During that trip I had audiences with President Nasser of Egypt, President Nyerere of Tanzania, President Jomo Kenyatta (who was then prime minister) of Kenya, Prime Minister Milton Obote of Uganda, President Azikiwe of Nigeria, President Nkrumah of Ghana, and President Sékou Touré of Guinea. I think the highlights were the audiences I had with those persons because it gave me a chance to sample their thinking. I was impressed by their analysis of the problem, and many of the suggestions they gave went a long way toward broadening my own outlook.

YOUNG SOCIALIST: How much influence does revolutionary Africa have on the thinking of Black people in this country?

MALCOLM X: All the influence in the world. You can't separate the militancy that's displayed on the African continent from the militancy that's displayed right here among American Blacks. The positive image that is developing of Africans is also developing in the minds of Black Americans, and consequently they develop a more positive image of themselves. Then they take more positive steps—actions.

So you can't separate the African revolution from the mood of the Black man in America. Neither could the colonization of Africa be separated from the menial position that the Black man in this country was satisfied to stay in for so long. Since Africa has gotten its independence through revolution, you'll notice the stepped-up cry against discrimination that has appeared in the Black community.

YOUNG SOCIALIST: How do you view the role of the U.S. in the Congo?

MALCOLM X: As criminal. Probably there is no better example of criminal activity against an oppressed people than the role the U.S. has been playing in the Congo, through her ties with Tshombe and the mercenaries. You can't overlook the fact that Tshombe gets his money from the U.S. The money he uses to hire these mercenaries—these paid killers imported from South Africa—comes from the United States. The pilots that fly these planes have been trained by the U.S. The bombs themselves that are blowing apart the bodies of women and children come from the U.S. So I can only view the role of the United States in the Congo as a criminal role. And I think the seeds she is sowing in the Congo she will have to harvest. The chickens that she has turned loose over there have got to come home to roost.

YOUNG SOCIALIST: What about the U.S. role in South Vietnam?

MALCOLM X: The same thing. It shows the real ignorance of those who control the American power structure. If France, with all types of heavy arms, as deeply entrenched as she was in what then was called Indochina, couldn't stay there, I don't see how anybody in their right mind can think the U.S. can get in there—it's impossible. So it shows her ignorance, her blindness, her lack of foresight and hindsight; and her complete defeat in South Vietnam is only a matter of time.

YOUNG SOCIALIST: How do you view the activity of white and Black students who went to the South last summer and attempted to register Black people to vote?

MALCOLM X: The attempt was good—I should say the objective to register Black people in the South was good because the only real power a poor man in this country has is the power of the ballot. But I don't believe sending them in and telling them to be nonviolent was intelligent. I go along with the effort toward registration, but I think they should be permitted to use whatever means at their disposal to defend themselves from the attacks of the Klan, the White Citizens' Council, and other groups.

YOUNG SOCIALIST: What do you think of the murder of the three civil rights workers and what's happened to their killers?[32]

MALCOLM X: It shows that the society we live in is not actually what it tries to represent itself as to the rest of the world. This was murder and the federal government is helpless because the case involves Negroes. Even the whites involved, were involved in helping Negroes. And concerning anything in this society involved in helping Negroes, the federal government shows an inability to function. But it can function in South Vietnam, in the Congo, in Berlin,[33] and in other places where it has no business. But it can't function in Mississippi.

YOUNG SOCIALIST: In a recent speech you mentioned that you met John Lewis of SNCC in Africa.[34] Do you feel that the younger and more militant leaders in the South are broadening their views on the whole general struggle?

MALCOLM X: Sure. When I was in the Black Muslim movement I spoke on many white campuses and Black campuses. I knew back in 1961 and '62 that the younger generation was much different from the older, and that many students were more sincere in their analysis of the problem and their desire to see the problem solved. In foreign countries the students have helped bring about revolution—it was the students who brought about the revolution in the Sudan, who swept Syngman Rhee out of office in Korea, swept Menderes out in Turkey. The students didn't think in terms of the odds against them, and they couldn't be bought out.

In America students have been noted for involving themselves in panty raids, goldfish swallowing, seeing how many can get in a telephone booth—not for their revolutionary political ideas or their desire to change unjust conditions. But some students are becoming more like their brothers around the world. However, the students have been deceived somewhat in what's known as the civil rights struggle (which was never designed to solve the problem). The students were maneuvered in the direction of thinking the problem was already analyzed, so they didn't try to analyze it for themselves.

In my thinking, if the students in this country forgot the analysis that has been presented to them, and they went into a huddle and began to research this problem of racism for themselves, independent of politicians and independent of all the foundations (which are a part of the power structure), and did it themselves, then some of their findings would be shocking, but they would see that they would never be able to bring about a solution to racism in their country as long as they're relying on the government to do it.

The federal government itself is just as racist as the government in Mississippi, and is more guilty of perpetuating the racist system. At the federal level they are more shrewd, more skillful at doing it, just like the FBI is more skillful than the state police and the state police are more skillful than the local police.

The same with politicians. The politician at the federal level is usually more skilled than the politician at the local level, and when he wants to practice racism, he's more skilled in the practice of it than those who practice it at the local level.

YOUNG SOCIALIST: What is your opinion of the Democratic Party?

MALCOLM X: The Democratic Party is responsible for the racism that exists in this country, along with the Republican Party. The leading racists in this country are Democrats. Goldwater isn't the leading racist—he's a racist but not the leading racist.[35] The racists who have influence in Washington, D.C., are Democrats. If you check, whenever any kind of legislation is suggested to mitigate the injustices that Negroes suffer in this country, you will find that the people who line up against it are members of Lyndon B. Johnson's party. The Dixiecrats are Democrats. The Dixiecrats are only a subdivision of the Democratic Party, and the same man over the Democrats is over the Dixiecrats.[36]

YOUNG SOCIALIST: What contribution can youth, especially

students, who are disgusted with racism in this society, make to the Black struggle for freedom?

MALCOLM X: Whites who are sincere don't accomplish anything by joining Negro organizations and making them integrated. Whites who are sincere should organize among themselves and figure out some strategy to break down the prejudice that exists in white communities. This is where they can function more intelligently and more effectively, in the white community itself, and this has never been done.

YOUNG SOCIALIST: What part in the world revolution are youth playing, and what lessons may this have for American youth?

MALCOLM X: If you've studied the captives being caught by the American soldiers in South Vietnam, you'll find that these guerrillas are young people. Some of them are just children and some haven't yet reached their teens. Most are teenagers. It is the teenagers abroad, all over the world, who are actually involving themselves in the struggle to eliminate oppression and exploitation. In the Congo, the refugees point out that many of the Congolese revolutionaries are children. In fact, when they shoot captive revolutionaries, they shoot all the way down to seven years old—that's been reported in the press. Because the revolutionaries are children, young people. In these countries the young people are the ones who most quickly identify with the struggle and the necessity to eliminate the evil conditions that exist. And here in this country, it has been my own observation that when you get into a conversation on racism and discrimination and segregation, you will find young people are more incensed over it—they feel more filled with an urge to eliminate it.

I think young people here can find a powerful example in the young *simbas* [lions] in the Congo and the young fighters in South Vietnam.

Another point: as the dark-skinned nations of this earth

become independent, as they develop and become stronger, that means that time is on the side of the American Negro. At this point the American Negro is still hospitable and friendly and forgiving. But if he is continually tricked and deceived and so on, and if there is still no solution to his problems, he will become completely disillusioned, disenchanted, and disassociate himself from the interest of America and its society. Many have done that already.

YOUNG SOCIALIST: What is your opinion of the worldwide struggle now going on between capitalism and socialism?

MALCOLM X: It is impossible for capitalism to survive, primarily because the system of capitalism needs some blood to suck. Capitalism used to be like an eagle, but now it's more like a vulture. It used to be strong enough to go and suck anybody's blood whether they were strong or not. But now it has become more cowardly, like the vulture, and it can only suck the blood of the helpless. As the nations of the world free themselves, then capitalism has less victims, less to suck, and it becomes weaker and weaker. It's only a matter of time in my opinion before it will collapse completely.

YOUNG SOCIALIST: What is the outlook for the Negro struggle in 1965?

MALCOLM X: Bloody. It was bloody in 1963, it was bloody in 1964, and all of the causes that created this bloodshed still remain. The March on Washington was designed to serve as a vent or valve for the frustration that produced this explosive atmosphere.[37] In 1964 they used the civil rights bill as a valve. What can they use in 1965? There is no trick that the politicians can use to contain the explosiveness that exists right here in Harlem.

And look at New York Police Commissioner Murphy. He's coming out in headlines trying to make it a crime now to even predict that there's going to be trouble.[38] This shows the caliber of American thinking. There's going to be an explosion, but don't talk about it. All the ingredients that produce explosions exist, but don't talk about it, he says. That's like saying 700 million Chinese don't exist.[39] This is the same approach. The American has become so guilt-ridden and filled with fear that instead of facing the reality of any situation, he pretends the situation doesn't exist. You know, in this country it's almost a crime to say there's a place called China—unless you mean that little island called Formosa. By the same token, it's almost a crime to say that people in Harlem are going to explode because the social dynamite that existed last year is still here.

So I think 1965 will be most explosive—more explosive than it was in '64 and '63. There's nothing they can do to contain it. The Negro leaders have lost their control over the people. So that when the people begin to explode—and their explosion is justified, not unjustified—the Negro leaders can't contain it.

Two interviews

He spoke the truth to our generation of revolutionists

Malcolm X at airport before leaving Ghana, May, 17, 1964.

"Robert Penn Warren interviewed a man named Malcolm X in June 1964, and I interviewed a man with the same name in January 1965. I phrase it that way because, after reading Warren's account, I almost wondered if we had interviewed the same man."

Two interviews

by Jack Barnes

The following article, marking the one-year anniversary of the assassination of Malcolm X, first appeared in the February 21, 1966, issue of the Militant.

Robert Penn Warren interviewed a man named Malcolm X in June, 1964, and I helped to interview a man with the same name in January 1965. I phrase it that way because, after reading Warren's account, I almost wondered if we had interviewed the same man. Of course, the difference was really in the interviewers, in their attitudes and assumptions.

Warren[40] was born and raised in the South and, as a young man, believed in segregation. He has spent much of his life in the North as a writer and teacher, and is now against segregation. Stirred by the Negro upsurge, he wanted to find out more about what Negroes think. So he set out to interview many of them for his book, *Who Speaks for the Negro?* (Random House, 1965).

His approach is that of a liberal. One of his favorite questions of the people he interviewed was did they think that it would have been a good idea to have compensated the Confederate slaveholders for the slaves emancipated; he seemed to hit it off best with those who said it would have been a good idea. He evidently was smart enough to omit this question with Malcolm, or at least he doesn't mention it.

Warren goes to the Hotel Theresa in Harlem for his interview with Malcolm. "I am admitted by a strong-looking young Negro man, dressed impeccably . . . ; he is silent but watchful, smooth-faced, impassive, of ominous dignity." (Not being a poet, as is Warren, I find it hard to conceive a dignity that is "ominous.") Malcolm shakes Warren's hand, "with the slightest hint of a smile." Warren looks him over:

"The most striking thing, at first, about that face is a sort of stoniness, a rigidity, as though beyond all feeling. When the lips move to speak you experience a faint hint of surprise. When—as I discover later—he scores a point and the face suddenly breaks into his characteristic wide, leering, merciless smile, with the powerful even teeth gleaming beyond the very pale pink lips, the effect is, to say the least, startling. But beyond the horn-rimmed glasses always the eyes are watching, pale brown or hazel, some tint of yellow. You cannot well imagine them closed in sleep."

"After the handshake, he turns to his aide. . . . I am, for the moment, dismissed, and wander across the room, inspecting it." ". . . as he stands there across the expanse of bare, ill-swept floor, conferring with the ominous attendant . . . I am watching him, and he knows I am watching him, but he gives no sign." Malcolm's failure to give a sign that he knows Warren is watching him is clearly as sinister as the "attendant" has now become.

"Finally" Malcolm beckons Warren into the tiny room used as his office. "Malcolm X tells me that he has only a few minutes, that he has found that you waste a lot of time with reporters and then you don't get much space." And so the interview begins.

It seemed somewhat different when Barry Sheppard and I interviewed Malcolm in the same office on January 18, 1965, a month before his assassination. Our interview was taped for the *Young Socialist*.

The thing that struck me first was how tired Malcolm looked. (In the *Autobiography*, Alex Haley describes the eighteen-hour schedule he followed.) At one point toward the end of the interview, a yawn can be heard on the tape, followed by the apology, "Excuse my tired mind." We were a little uncomfortable at first, feeling that Malcolm might need rest more urgently than we needed an interview and, because this was the first time we had met, there was some over-politeness on both sides. Malcolm sent out for coffee for the three of us, making his familiar joke about his preference for light coffee, and after that the atmosphere warmed up.

After the formal interview, we offered to type it up and bring it back, edited to fit our space requirements, for his final check and corrections. I also asked him if he would like the Young Socialist Alliance to organize a national speaking tour of campuses for him later in the year. He expressed interest in this, but did not commit himself, saying he would discuss it the next time we got together.

Let us return to poor Warren. He tries to catch Malcolm in a contradiction, but Malcolm deftly avoids the trap, and makes his own point. Warren's reaction:

"I discovered that that pale, dull yellowish face that had seemed so veiled, so stony, as though beyond all feeling, had flashed into its merciless, leering life—the sudden wolfish grin, the pale pink lips drawn hard back to show the strong teeth, the unveiled glitter of the eyes beyond the lenses, giving the sense that the lenses were only part of a clever disguise, that the eyes needed no help, that they suddenly see everything."

Malcolm had ruined his eyes reading by poor light at night while he was in prison, and says in the *Autobiography* that he had astigmatism. Never mind the facts—Warren senses "that the lenses were only part of a clever disguise" (an elaborate scheme for fooling liberals somehow). Warren didn't really need to look into Malcolm's eyes—he came to the interview convinced that Malcolm was racist, demagogic, and opportunist ("He may end at the barricades, or in Congress. Or he might even end on the board of a bank"), and that is what he went away with.

Malcolm knew the white liberal type very well, and he must have had to grin ("leer") when he saw how closely Warren was conforming to the type. And when Warren asks Malcolm "if he believes in political assassination" (!), it is not hard to see why Malcolm might "turn the hard, impassive face and veiled eyes" upon Warren and say, "I wouldn't know anything about that."

I returned to Malcolm's office less than a week after our interview, bearing the edited transcript Barry had made from the tape. (If we had known this would be the last thing we would get from him, we of course would not have shortened the transcript, even slightly.) Malcolm was talking to a young man in his inner office. While I waited, for about ten minutes, one of Malcolm's co-workers, the only other person in the outer office, dozed at a reception desk.

A small stack of *Militant*s lay on the desk with a couple of dimes on top.

As Malcolm read the transcript, he began to smile. When he came to the question about capitalism and the statement, "It's only a matter of time in my opinion before it will collapse completely," he said, "This is the farthest I've ever gone. They will go wild over this." I asked if he wanted to tone it down and, without hesitation, he answered no.

He said he felt the editing had sharpened up what he had

originally said; that he had been tired when he gave the interview. He made very few changes and I said that would be the final copy, just as he had left it. He said, "Make any additional changes you want—it's fine. This is the kind of editing it's a pleasure to read." The *Young Socialist* made no changes. The interview appeared as Malcolm had read and approved.

Malcolm then began to talk about young revolutionaries he had met and been impressed by in Africa and Europe. He said he had a long list of them—he called them "contacts"—and would give me a copy so we could send them the issue of the *Young Socialist* that contained his interview. He also spoke about the *Militant*, and how often he had seen it abroad.

I told him I might be going to Algeria for the World Youth Festival (then scheduled for the summer of 1965) and might be able to meet some of his contacts there.[41] He said, "Great, that would be a good experience; they have a hard time believing that revolutionaries exist in the United States." We arranged that he would give me the list after the *Young Socialist* came off the press.

I reminded him about our proposal for a national campus tour. This time he responded very favorably; he must have thought about it further and may have discussed it with some of his co-workers. He said he had learned from much experience of speaking on campus that youth were in general the only whites that seemed to be open-minded. He said he was sure that the government would try to buy off the white students who were radical, that this was their main problem. He said they should "get in a closet"—away from the professors and the job offers from government and business—and think out their ideas more thoroughly and basically. They could travel the road before them in one of two ways, he said, "—as missionaries or as revolutionaries."

He asked a lot of questions about the Young Socialist Alliance—how many locals, where, what campuses? He wanted to know how long the tour would last; he said he could not make it until after his return from another trip abroad that he was committed to make, but that would be the best time. I said I was sure that on most campuses we would be able to get broader sponsorship than the YSA for his speeches, and he said he didn't care how broad or how narrow the sponsorship would be.

He asked me if I read French and then gave me a magazine from Paris with a story about his talk there in November, 1964.[42] He said he thought it was a communist magazine, and that "things are very different in Europe and Africa. There are communists and socialists all over, and no one makes a big deal out of it. They can't imagine how narrow-minded this country is."

Malcolm also spoke at some length about imperialism, along what Marxists might call Luxemburgian lines—how the West is in a real bind because the colonial revolution is cutting off places where imperialism can expand.

I felt completely at ease with Malcolm throughout this discussion, which lasted quite a while at his initiative. He grew quite excited at the thought of his African youth contacts getting the *Young Socialist* interview and at the possibility of my meeting them. I had no sense of "taking" his valuable time—he was giving it voluntarily, and not out of mere politeness.

It is inconceivable that he would be like that with a liberal. There would be no common points of departure, no common projects of any kind, for him to discuss with a liberal who felt, as Warren did, that he was accomplishing his mission when he got Malcolm to "admit" that he didn't "see in the American system the possibility of self-regeneration."

Malcolm X arriving at London airport, February 9, 1965, after being refused entry into France, where he had visited and spoken the previous November.

Malcolm X addressing young civil rights fighters in Selma, Alabama,
February 4, 1965, during struggle over the right to register to vote.

*"Malcolm X was to us the face and authentic voice
of the forces of the American revolution."*

He spoke the truth
to our generation of revolutionists

by Jack Barnes, March 5, 1965

The following are excerpts from the talk by Jack Barnes on be-half of the Young Socialist Alliance at a memorial meeting for Malcolm X attended by more than 200 people organized by the Militant Labor Forum at its hall in Lower Manhattan. Other speakers included Malcolm's close collaborator James Shabazz; Farrell Dobbs, national secretary of the Socialist Workers Party; and Robert DesVerney, a writer for the Militant. *The meeting was chaired by 1964 SWP presidential candidate Clifton DeBerry.*

I would like to speak tonight not only for the socialist youth of the Young Socialist Alliance, but also for the young revolutionists in our movement around the world who would want to speak at a memorial for Malcolm X but who cannot be here. This is especially true of those in Africa, the Middle East, France, and England, who recently had a chance to see and hear Malcolm.

Malcolm was the leader of the struggle for Black liberation. He was, as stated at his funeral by Ossie Davis, the Black shining prince, the manhood of the Harlems of the world. To his people he first and foremost belongs.

But he was also the teacher, inspirer, and leader of a much smaller group, the revolutionary socialist youth of America. He was to us the face and the authentic voice of the forces of the American revolution. And above all, he spoke the truth for our generation of revolutionists.

What attracted revolutionary youth to Malcolm X? More important, what often made youth—including youth who are not Black—who listened to him revolutionists? I think there were two main things. First, he spoke the simple truth—unadorned, unvarnished, and uncompromising. Second was the evolution and content of Malcolm's political thought.

Malcolm saw the depth of the hypocrisy and falsehood that covers the real social relations that make up American society. To him the key was not so much the lies that the ruling class and its spokesmen propagated, but the lies and the falsehoods about his people—their past and their potentialities—which they accepted.

Malcolm's message to the ghetto, his agitation against racism, was a special kind. What he had to say and what he did stemmed from a study of the history of the Afro-Americans. He explained that in order for Black Americans to know what to do—to know how to go about winning freedom—they had to first answer three questions: Where did you come from? How did you get here? Who is responsible for your condition?

Malcolm's truth was so explosive because it stemmed from a careful study of how the Afro-American was enslaved. He publicized the facts that have been suppressed from the regular history books and kept out of the schools.

While in the Black Muslims and after he left, Malcolm taught that the process by which the Africans were made into slaves was one of dehumanizing them. Through barbarous cruelty, comparable to the worst Nazi concentration camps, they were taught to fear the white man. They were systematically stripped of their language, culture, history, names, religion, of all connections with their home in Africa—of their identity. They were named Negro, signifying this lack of identity and this denial of their African origin.

Especially after their "emancipation" they were taught the Christianity of meekness and submission and of their reward in heaven. They were taught that Africa was a jungle where people lived in mud huts, and that the white man had done them a great favor in bringing them to America.

Malcolm asked the Black American: Who taught you to hate yourself? Who taught you to be a pacifist? Was he a pacifist? Who said Black people cannot defend themselves? Does he defend himself? Who taught you not to go too far and too fast in your fight for freedom? Did he stand to lose something by the speed of your victory? Who taught you to vote for the fox to escape the wolf? What does the fox give you in return?

All these questions, and so many more, needed no answers. All the questions were directed to those who had nothing to lose and no stake in the system as it exists now.

His political thought was the other important factor in the development of those who were taught by him. First, he believed in and explained the need for Afro-American unity. He felt it was necessary to base your alliances on your own unity, and reject unconditionally any degrading or compromising alliances. It is only upon the basis of this unity, and the dignity and self-respect that goes along with it, that the battle for freedom can be waged. Those who would bypass this step would condemn the Black Americans to be a tail to the kite of other, more conservative forces.

"We cannot think of uniting with others, until after we have first united among ourselves. We cannot think of being acceptable to others until we have first proven acceptable to ourselves. One can't unite bananas with scattered leaves."[43] Malcolm knew that Afro-Americans had had enough of this kind of unity—with the liberals, the Communist Party, and the Socialist Party.

Secondly, he spoke of self-defense, and the real meaning of violence. He continually pointed out that the source of violence was the oppressor, not the oppressed. He continually pointed to the use of violence by the oppressor. Out of one side of its mouth the government and press preach pacifism to the American Negro, while out of the other side comes the cold announcement that they will destroy as many North Vietnamese as they wish. Malcolm never tired of pointing out the hypocrisy of this form of pacifism, its ineffectuality and its degrading and belittling character.

Malcolm told us, at the first Militant Labor Forum at which he spoke, that "if George Washington didn't get independence for this country nonviolently, and if Patrick Henry didn't come up with a nonviolent statement, and you taught me to look upon them as patriots and heroes, then it's time for you to realize that I have studied your books well. . . . No white person would go about fighting for freedom in the same manner that he has helped me and you to fight for our freedom. No, none of them would. When it comes to Black freedom, then the white man freedom-rides and sits in, he's nonviolent, he sings, 'We Shall Overcome,' and all that stuff. But when the property of the white man is threatened, or the freedom of the white man is threatened, he's not nonviolent."[44]

Thirdly, unlike any other Black leader, and unlike any other mass leader in my lifetime, he continually exposed the real role of the Democratic Party, and pointed to the mistake in believing the federal government of this country would free the Afro-American. He said, "The Democrats get Negro support, yet the Negroes get nothing in return. The Negroes put the Democrats first, yet the Democrats put the Negroes last. And the alibi that the Democrats use—they blame the Dixiecrats. A Dixiecrat is nothing but a Democrat in disguise. . . . Because Dixie in reality means all that territory south of the Canadian border."[45]

Malcolm X always sought to expose those who were really responsible for maintaining the racism of this society rather than directing his fire at the puppets. When New York Police Commissioner Murphy attacked him and others as "irresponsible," Malcolm responded that Murphy was only doing his job. Mayor Wagner, Murphy's boss, was the one responsible for the charge, he said.

Malcolm never tired of explaining and demonstrating that it was the federal government headed by President [Lyndon] Johnson that was responsible for maintaining racism in the North and South. In doing this he showed the continuity of the inhuman treatment of Negroes and the responsibility of those who run this society for the condition of the Black people. As one of his comrades, Brother Benjamin, pointed out at a recent meeting of the Organization of Afro-American Unity, the North is responsible for the racism in the South, because "they won the Civil War."

It was in talking about the Democratic Party that another aspect of Malcolm came clearly to the fore. This was his ability to translate the complex and important ideas which he developed and absorbed into the language of those he knew would change the world. The ability to speak clearly to the oppressed has been the unique genius of all great revolutionary leaders in history.

The [June 1, 1964] *Militant* reported that Malcolm, at his press conference, spoke of President Johnson as being hypocritical. He pointed out that LBJ's closest friend in the Senate, Richard Russell, was leading the fight against the civil rights bill. Malcolm was challenged by a reporter who doubted that Johnson's friendship with Russell proved anything. Malcolm looked at him with his usual smile and said, off the cuff, "If you tell me you're against robbing banks and your best friend is Jesse James, I have grounds to doubt your sincerity."

The final point in his political development that was so important for the education of those young people who followed him, looked to him, or in many ways were educated by him, was his revolutionary internationalism.

Malcolm gave at least three reasons for his internationalist outlook. First was the common identity of the power structure which practiced racism in this country and which practiced imperialism abroad. "This system is not only ruling us in America, it is ruling the world," he said.

Second, only through Afro-Americans realizing that they were part of a great majority of nonwhites in the world who were fighting for and winning freedom would they have the courage to fight the battle for freedom with whatever means necessary.

Malcolm said that "among the so-called Negroes in this country, as a rule the civil rights groups, those who believe in civil rights, they spend most of their time trying to prove they are Americans. Their thinking is usually domestic, confined to the boundaries of America, and they always look upon themselves . . . upon the American stage, the American stage is a white stage. So a Black man standing on that stage in America automatically is in the minority. He is the underdog, and in his struggle he always uses an approach that is a begging, hat-in-hand, compromising approach." But, he said: We don't beg, we don't thank you for giving us what you should have given us a hundred years ago.[46]

Last, was the fact that in the final analysis freedom could only be won in one place when it was won everywhere. In Africa, he said, "Our problem is your problem. . . . Your problems will never be fully solved until and unless ours are solved. You will never be fully respected until and unless we are also respected. You will never be recognized as free human beings until and unless we are also recognized and treated as human beings."[47]

Though Malcolm X came from the American ghetto, spoke for the American ghetto, and directed his message to the American ghetto first of all, he is a figure of world importance, and developed his ideas in relation to the great events of world history in his time.

If Malcolm X is to be compared with any international figure, the most striking parallel is with Fidel Castro. Both of them belong to the generation that was shaped ideologically under the twin circumstances of World War II and the monstrous betrayals and defaults of Stalinized Communist parties. These men found their way independently to the revolutionary struggle, bypassing both Social Democracy and Stalinism.

Each started from the struggle of his own oppressed people for liberation. Each embraced the nationalism of his people as necessary to mobilize them to struggle for their freedom. Each stressed the importance of the solidarity of the oppressed all over the world in their struggle against a common oppressor.

Fidel did not start out as a thoroughgoing Marxist or as a revolutionary socialist. Like Malcolm, he was determined to pursue the national liberation of his people by "whatever means necessary" and without any compromises with those with any stake in the status quo.

Fidel Castro's dedication to political independence and to economic development for Cuba led him eventually to opposition to capitalism. So, also, Malcolm's uncompromising stand against racism brought him to identify with the revolutions of the colonial people who were turning against capitalism, and finally to conclude that the elimination of capitalism in this country was necessary for freedom. Just as Fidel Castro discovered that there can be no political independence and economic development in a colonial country without breaking from capitalism, so Malcolm had come to the conclusion that capitalism and racism were so entangled in the United States that you had to uproot the system in order to eliminate racism.

Malcolm's Black nationalism was aimed at preparing Black people to struggle for their freedom. "The greatest mistake of the movement," he said in an interview in the February 25 *Village Voice,* "has been trying to organize a sleeping people around specific goals. You have to wake the people up first, then you'll get action."

"Wake them up to their exploitation?" the interviewer asked.

"No, to their humanity, to their own worth, and to their heritage," he answered.[48]

Everything he said to the Black people was designed to raise their confidence, to organize them independently of those who oppressed them, to teach them who was responsible for their condition and who their allies were. He explained that they were part of the great majority—the nonwhites and the oppressed of the world. He taught that freedom could be won only by fighting for it; it has never been given to anyone. He explained that it could be won only by making a real revolution that uproots and changes the entire society.

Thus it is not surprising that many who considered themselves socialists, radicals, and even Marxists could not recognize and identify with Malcolm's revolutionary character. They could not recognize the revolutionary content of this great leader clothed in the new forms, language, and dark colors of the American proletarian ghetto.

Even with all his uniqueness and greatness as an individual, he could not have reached this understanding unless the conditions in this country were such that it was possible. Even though no one can fill his shoes, the fact that he did what he did, developed as the revolutionary leader he was, is the proof of more Malcolms to come.

He was a proof as Fidel was a proof. Fidel stood up ninety miles away from the most powerful imperialism in the world and thumbed his nose and showed us, "See, it can be done. They can't go on controlling the world forever."

Malcolm went even further than Fidel, because Malcolm challenged American capitalism from right inside. He was the living proof for our generation of revolutionists that it can and will happen here.

Our job, the job of the YSA, is to teach the revolutionary youth of this country to tell the difference between the nationalism of the oppressed and the nationalism of the oppressor, to teach them to differentiate the forces of liberation from the forces of the exploiters; to teach them to hear the voices of the revolution regardless of the forms they take; to teach them to differentiate between the self-defense of the victim and violence of the aggressor; to teach them to refuse to give an inch to white liberalism and to reach out to Malcolm's heirs, the vanguard of the ghetto, as brothers and comrades.

NOTES

1. An account by Malcolm X of his trip to Ghana can be found in *The Autobiography of Malcolm X* (New York: Ballantine, 1973).

2. Some thirty former colonies in Africa had won political independence between 1956 and 1964. In southern Africa, however, Angola and Mozambique remained Portuguese colonies, Southern Rhodesia (today Zimbabwe) was still under British colonial domination South-West Africa (today Namibia) was ruled by South Africa, and the white-supremacist apartheid system still held sway in South Africa itself.

Angola won its independence from Portugal in 1975. Almost immediately it was invaded by forces in South Africa's white minority apartheid regime, which, with Washington's backing, launched military assaults against Angola over the next thirteen years aimed at overturning the government there. South Africa's aims in Southern Africa were defeated in 1988 when volunteer Cuban troops—invited into the country at the request of the government of Angola—joined Angolan and Namibian forces in crushing the apartheid army at the battle of Cuito Cuanavale in southern Angola. The outcome of that battle gave impetus to the liberation forces in the region, leading shortly thereafter to Namibia's independence from South African colonial rule and by 1994 the downfall of the apartheid regime itself. See Nelson Mandela and Fidel Castro, *How Far We Slaves Have Come! South Africa and Cuba in Today's World* (New York: Pathfinder, 1991).

3. The most well-known victim of this practice was the singer Paul Robeson. Another important case was that of Black journalist William Worthy, who had to fight a two-year legal battle to overturn a 1962 conviction for visiting Cuba after he had been denied a passport.

4. In May 1964 New York's daily newspapers ran lurid stories about the existence of a gang of young Blacks, allegedly calling themselves "Blood Brothers," that had supposedly been organized by dissident Black Muslims to attack whites. For the talk on this subject given by Malcolm X on his return to the United States, see "The Harlem 'Hate-Gang' Scare," in *Malcolm X Speaks* (New York: Pathfinder, 1965, 1989).

5. On April 7, 1964, Rev. Bruce Klunder was crushed to death by a bulldozer during a civil rights demonstration at a school construction site in Cleveland.

6. The Congo declared its independence from Belgium June 30, 1960. The prime minister of the newly independent government of the Congo was Patrice Lumumba, who had led the liberation struggle there. Washington and Brussels moved swiftly to prepare the overthrow of the Lumumba government. In face of attacks by Belgian troops, units of mercenaries, and the forces of the imperialist-backed secessionist regime of Moise Tshombe in southern Katanga province, Lumumba took the fatal step of requesting military help from the United Nations. In September 1960 Congolese army officer Joseph Mobutu, at the instigation of Washington and Brussels, deposed Lumumba. Lumumba was later arrested and, as UN forces looked on, handed over to Tshombe's forces, who murdered the Congolese leader in January 1961.

In 1964 Tshombe was installed as prime minister of the central government in the Congo. Liberation-minded forces that looked to Lumumba, based in the country's eastern provinces, led a revolt. Mercenaries and Belgian troops aided Tshombe in crushing the uprising, as did Washington, which organized what the *New York Times* in 1966 called "an instant air force" of U.S. planes flown by U.S. pilots to carry out bombing and strafing missions. The U.S. Central Intelligence Agency also supplied pilots from the ranks of right-wing Cuban exiles it had financed and trained to carry out terrorist operations against the people and government of revolutionary Cuba.

7. The Civil Rights Act of 1964, signed into law by Pres. Lyndon B. Johnson on July 2, banned discrimination in voting, public fa-

cilities, schools, and employment. Two weeks earlier, three civil rights workers—two white, one Black—had disappeared in Philadelphia, Mississippi. The battered bodies of Michael Schwerner, Andrew Goodman, and James E. Chaney were found on August 4. At the time of the Oxford Union debate the FBI had still made no arrests.

8. Ruling on a case called *Brown v. Board of Education*, the U.S. Supreme Court declared in 1954 that segregated school systems, which it had previously upheld as lawful, were in violation of the Constitution.

9. On July 16, 1964, a fifteen-year-old Black youth, James Powell, was shot and killed by a New York police officer. Two days later, cops broke up a demonstration at a central Harlem police station demanding the officer's arrest, and the organizers were arrested. Police then rampaged through the area, beating, arresting, and shooting residents, killing one. The ensuing rebellion in Harlem and the predominantly Black community of Bedford-Stuyvesant in Brooklyn lasted five days.

10. Four days before Malcolm X spoke, President Johnson announced a massive escalation of the war against Vietnam, including sustained bombing of North Vietnam and a big increase in U.S. combat troops. By the end of July, there were 75,000 U.S. troops in Vietnam.

11. In 1954 the French army suffered a decisive defeat at the hands of Vietnamese liberation forces at Dien Bien Phu. The U.S. government moved in to replace France as the dominant imperialist power in the region, propping up a subservient regime in South Vietnam.

12. Ian Smith was the prime minister of the white-minority regime administering the British colony of Southern Rhodesia.

13. In April 1955 representatives of twenty-nine countries of Africa and Asia met in Bandung, Indonesia. The conference approved a final communiqué opposing "racial segregation and discrimination . . . in large regions of Africa and in other parts of the world," and declaring colonialism "an evil which should speedily be brought to an end."

14. The December 31, 1962, issue of *Look* details four days of secret negotiations in late September of that year to arrange a staged

confrontation in which Gov. Ross Barnett was to be seen blocking Meredith from entering the university to register. Barnett would then step aside when federal marshals drew their guns. The deal fell through, however. Barnett's segregationist demagogy inflamed the racist mobs he had helped mobilize, and President Kennedy was forced to send in 2,500 federal troops to establish control.

15. The Emancipation Proclamation went into effect January 1, 1863, freeing slaves in the Southern states that were in rebellion against the federal government in the U.S. Civil War.

16. Medgar Evers, a leader of the National Association for the Advancement of Colored People (NAACP) in Mississippi, was assassinated in front of his home on June 12, 1963. On Sunday morning, September 15, 1963, a bomb exploded in Birmingham, Alabama, in the Sixteenth Street Baptist Church, which had been the staging point for desegregation demonstrations. Eleven-year-old Denise McNair and fourteen-year-olds Cynthia Wesley, Carole Robertson, and Addie Mae Collins were killed by the bomb and about twenty were injured.

17. The Great Society was the term used by President Johnson in his January 1965 State of the Union speech to Congress to refer to his domestic program.

18. White Citizens' Councils were racist organizations formed in the South in the mid-1950s to carry out night-riding attacks and other terrorist activity against Blacks in response to growing demands to desegregate schools and other public facilities.

19. The Big Six was a term used by the mass media to refer to a number of the most prominent figures in the civil rights movement. These were A. Philip Randolph, founding leader of the Negro American Labor Council; Martin Luther King, Jr., of the Southern Christian Leadership Conference (SCLC); Roy Wilkins of the NAACP; James Farmer of the Congress of Racial Equality (CORE); Whitney Young of the Urban League; and John Lewis of the Student Nonviolent Coordinating Committee (SNCC).

20. Hideki Tojo was prime minister of Japan during most of World War II.

21. On August 8, 1963, Mao Zedong, chairman of the Chinese

Communist Party, made a statement calling on "persons of all colors in the world . . . to unite against the racial discrimination practiced by U.S. imperialism and to support American Negroes in their struggle against racial discrimination."

22. The Mississippi Freedom Democratic Party, formed in April 1964, had tried without success at the Democrats' August 1964 national convention to obtain the ouster of delegates from Mississippi's segregationist Democratic organization. The MFDP then announced its own candidates for the November voting and conducted a Freedom Election open to all Mississippi residents, registered or not. After the elections, Fannie Lou Hamer toured the North as part of an MFDP team that denounced the exclusion of Blacks from the official Mississippi voting and called on Congress not to seat those elected. Malcolm X's speech to the December 20, 1964, rally in Harlem during a national tour by Hamer is printed in the chapter "With Mrs. Fannie Lou Hamer," in *Malcolm X Speaks.*

23. On January 4, 1965, the U.S. Congress was to begin a new session. Many civil rights and other organizations were supporting the MFDP demand that Congress refuse to seat the winners in the elections in Mississippi, from which Black voters had been excluded.

24. The OAAU's Basic Unity Program of February 15, 1965, is contained in Malcolm X, *February 1965: The Final Speeches* (New York: Pathfinder, 1992), pp. 269–81. Its founding statement, dated June 28, 1964, can be found in George Breitman, *The Last Year of Malcolm X: The Evolution of a Revolutionary* (New York: Pathfinder, 1967), pp. 115–22.

25. COFO was the Council of Federated Organizations, a coalition of civil rights groups in Mississippi formed in 1961.

26. Malcolm X is referring to the Black Muslim leadership's refusal to respond to an attack against its members by Los Angeles police in 1962. On April 27 of that year, police shot seven unarmed Black Muslims, killing one and crippling another for life. The cops then arrested sixteen Muslims on frame-up charges of assaulting the police. Malcolm X organized a broad defense campaign involving many Black community organizations in Los Angeles. As he was preparing to launch the campaign on a national scale, the Chicago

headquarters of the Nation of Islam called off the entire effort, restricting defense work to the courts. This episode is described in "The Split," in Breitman, *The Last Year of Malcolm X.*

27. Mau Mau was the name given by British colonial rulers to rebel groups that carried out an armed struggle during the 1950s for the independence of Kenya. The British authorities jailed Kenyatta in 1953 as a leader of that struggle.

28. Tshombe was in exile in Europe in 1963–64.

29. Manhattan congressman William Fitts Ryan announced December 23, 1964, that he would introduce a resolution to deny seats in the House of Representatives to the five Mississippi candidates declared elected in the official voting the previous month. Harlem congressman Adam Clayton Powell was one of sixteen other representatives supporting the resolution.

30. Malcolm X spoke in Tuskegee and Selma, Alabama, February 3 and 4. He was scheduled to speak in Mississippi later that month but was assassinated before he could make the trip.

31. For Malcolm X's view on Elijah Muhammad's moral corruption and hypocrisy, see his February 15 speech, "There's a Worldwide Revolution Going On," and February 18 radio interview, "The Black Muslim Movement: an Assessment," both in Malcolm X, *February 1965: The Final Speeches* (New York: Pathfinder, 1992).

32. In early December 1964, more than five months after the murder of the three civil rights workers in Mississippi, the FBI arrested twenty-one men. Charges were dismissed the following week because of "insufficient evidence." After three years of delay, seven were eventually convicted and sentenced to prison terms ranging from three to ten years.

33. During the 1960s, the United States maintained a garrison of more than five thousand troops in Berlin. In October 1961, U.S. and Soviet tanks had faced each other in a standoff across the newly built Berlin Wall in the heart of the occupied city.

34. Malcolm X spoke of his meeting with John Lewis at a January 7, 1965, meeting of the Militant Labor Forum. See *Malcolm X Speaks,* p. 231. Some comments by Lewis and another SNCC leader on the impact in Africa of Malcolm X's trip there can be found in

Malcolm X Speaks, pp. 101–2.

35. In the 1964 presidential election, the Republican candidate Barry Goldwater was defeated by the Democratic candidate Lyndon B. Johnson.

36. The Dixiecrats were the openly segregationist wing of the Democratic Party dominant at the time in most of the U.S. South.

37. The August 28, 1963, March on Washington drew more than 250,000 people for a rally at the Lincoln Memorial. The march called for passage of civil rights legislation then pending in Congress.

38. On January 10, 1965, New York Police Commissioner Michael J. Murphy sharply criticized Black leaders such as Malcolm X who had pointed to the mood of frustration in the Black ghettos and had predicted future outbreaks of resistance. It was such warnings, Murphy implied, that were causing the trouble.

39. Until the early 1970s, the U.S. government refused to recognize the People's Republic of China, maintaining instead that the capitalist government of Taiwan (Formosa) represented China.

40. Robert Penn Warren (1905–1989) was an American novelist, poet, and literary critic. He is the only writer to have won the Pulitzer Prize both for fiction and for poetry.

41. The Ninth World Youth Festival had been set for July 28–August 7, 1965, in Algiers, and the Young Socialist Alliance had asked Barnes to lead its delegation. Organizers of the festival postponed the event and began looking for another site following the June 1965 coup that overthrew the popular revolutionary government of Ahmed Ben Bella, which had offered to host the international youth gathering. Thirty-six years later the Fifteenth World Festival of Youth and Students was held in Algiers, August 8–16, 2001. Works by Malcolm X were among the biggest sellers at the Pathfinder book table during the Algiers gathering.

42. The question-and-answer period from that November 1964 talk appears under the title "At a Meeting in Paris," in *By Any Means Necessary* (New York: Pathfinder, 1970, 1992). The meeting was sponsored by the organization Présence Africaine, and the transcript was run in 1965 in the English-language edition of the magazine of the same name.

43. See "A Declaration of Independence," March 12, 1964, in *Malcolm X Speaks.*

44. See "Speech on Black Revolution," April 8, 1964, in *Two Speeches by Malcolm X* (New York: Pathfinder, 1965, 1990). This pamphlet contains the full text of Malcolm's talk. For the question period, see chapter two of *By Any Means Necessary.*

45. *Two Speeches by Malcolm X,* p. 23.

46. *Two Speeches by Malcolm X,* p. 18.

47. *Malcolm X Speaks,* p. 91. From a memorandum submitted by Malcolm X to the July 17–21, 1964, meeting of the Organization of African Unity in Cairo, Egypt.

48. See "We Have to Learn How to Think," an interview with Marlene Nadle for the *Village Voice,* in *February 1965: The Final Speeches.*

INDEX

Abrahams, Eric, 31

Africa, 32, 126; colonial domination of, 22, 55, 111, 139; identification with, 21, 57, 111; image of among U.S. Blacks, 23, 55, 56–57, 65–66, 99, 131; Malcolm X in, 10–11, 81, 109, 111; and neocolonialism, 59, 60–61; resources of, 22; support in for U.S. Blacks, 81–82, 96; unity of, 79–80, 88

African nationalism, 58, 59

African revolution, 52–53, 54–55, 58–59; and U.S. Black struggle, 55, 57, 59–60, 63, 65–66, 111. *See also* Congo

Algeria, 25, 81, 109, 111

Algerian revolution, 13; fall of, 145

Allies, 65–66, 79, 131–32, 136

Americanism, 11, 20; and term *American,* 20, 22, 56, 134

Angola, 20, 26, 54, 139

Apartheid, 32, 139

Attwood, William, 98, 102

Autobiography of Malcolm X, 123, 139

Azikiwe, Nnamdi, 81, 111

Bandung Conference (1955), 58, 141

Barnes, Jack, 14, 15, 107, 129

Barnett, Ross, 61–62, 142

Belgium, 37, 59, 140

Ben Bella, Ahmed, 25, 145

Berkeley, Humphry, 31

Berlin, 113, 144

Big Six, 76, 82, 142. *See also* Black leaders

Birmingham: church bombing in, 64, 142; 1963 struggle in, 63

Black communities, control of, 49, 91, 109

Black leaders, traditional, 24, 62, 76, 80, 82, 100, 132; losing control, 27, 60, 116, 117

Black Muslims. *See* Nation of Islam

Black nationalism, 13–14, 88–89, 109, 135, 136

Black politicians, 91, 92–93

Blacks: change in consciousness of, 65–66, 72, 83–84, 113; institutionalized oppression of, 41–42; second-class status of, 20, 26, 62–63, 75–76; self-image of, 23–24, 55–58, 65–66, 110, 111, 131; token gains by, 61, 62, 63, 75–79, 80. *See also* Africa; Racism, cause of

Black struggle: as part of world struggle, 65–66, 78–80, 81–82, 134–35, 136; violence vs., 22, 44, 48–49, 63–64, 142. *See also* Africa, support in for U.S. Blacks; African revolution, and U.S. Black struggle; Civil rights workers, 1964 murder of; Human rights, and civil rights

Britain, 36, 37; Blacks in, 48, 55–56; as colonial power, 26, 58–59. *See also* United Kingdom

"By any means necessary," 33, 40–41, 42, 44–45, 89, 109, 135

By Any Means Necessary (Malcolm X), 145

147

Che Guevara Talks to Young People

ERNESTO CHE GUEVARA

In eight talks between 1959 and 1964, the Argentine-born revolutionary challenges youth of Cuba and the world to read and to study. To work and become disciplined. To join the front lines of struggles, small and large. To aspire to be revolutionary combatants. To politicize their organizations and in the process politicize themselves. To become a different kind of human being as they strive together with working people of all lands to transform the world. And, along this line of march, to revel in the spontaneity and joy of being young. $14.95

The Working Class and the Transformation of Learning

The Fraud of Education Reform under Capitalism

JACK BARNES

"Until society is reorganized so that education is a human activity from the time we are very young until the time we die, there will be no education worthy of working, creating humanity." $3.00

Cuba and the Coming American Revolution

JACK BARNES

"There will be a victorious revolution in the United States before there will be a victorious counterrevolution in Cuba." That statement, made by Fidel Castro in 1961, remains as accurate today as when it was spoken. This is a book about the class struggle in the United States, where the revolutionary capacities of workers and farmers are today as utterly discounted by the ruling powers as were those of the Cuban toilers. And just as wrongly. It is about the example set by the people of Cuba that revolution is not only necessary—it can be made. $13.00

The Cuban Revolution

October 1962
The 'Missile' Crisis as Seen from Cuba

Tomás Diez Acosta

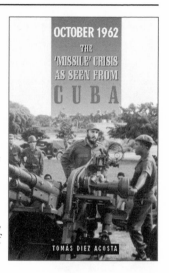

In October 1962, during what is widely known as the Cuban Missile Crisis, Washington pushed the world to the edge of nuclear war. Here, for the first time, the full story of that historic moment is told from the perspective of the Cuban people. Led by Cuba's revolutionary government, their determination to defend the country's sovereignty and their socialist revolution blocked U.S. plans for a military assault and opened the way to resolve the crisis, thus saving humanity from the consequences of a nuclear holocaust. $24.00

To Speak the Truth
Why Washington's 'Cold War' against Cuba Doesn't End

Fidel Castro and Che Guevara

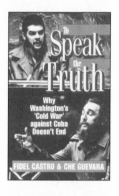

In historic speeches before the United Nations and UN bodies, Guevara and Castro address the workers of the world, explaining why the U.S. government so hates the example set by the socialist revolution in Cuba and why Washington's effort to destroy it will fail. $16.95

Playa Girón/Bay of Pigs
Washington's First Military Defeat in the Americas

Fidel Castro, José Ramón Fernández

In less than 72 hours of combat in April 1961, Cuba's revolutionary armed forces defeated an invasion by 1,500 mercenaries organized by Washington. In the process, the Cuban people set an example for workers, farmers, and youth throughout the world that with political consciousness, class solidarity, unflinching courage, and revolutionary leadership, it is possible to stand up to enormous might and seemingly insurmountable odds— and win. $20.00

By Malcolm X

February 1965: The Final Speeches
Speeches from the last three weeks of the life of this outstanding leader of the oppressed Black nationality and of the working class in the United States. A large part is material previously unavailable, with some in print for the first time. $18.95

By Any Means Necessary
Speeches tracing the evolution of Malcolm X's views on political alliances, women's rights, intermarriage, capitalism and socialism, and more. $15.95

Malcolm X on Afro-American History
Recounts the hidden history of the labor of people of African origin and their achievements. $10.95

Malcolm X Speaks
Speeches from the last year of Malcolm X's life tracing the evolution of his views on racism, capitalism, socialism, political action, and more. $17.95

Malcolm X: The Last Speeches
"Any kind of movement for freedom for Black people based solely within the confines of America is absolutely doomed to fail." Speeches and interviews from the last two years of his life. $16.95

Also:

Two Speeches by Malcolm X, $5.00
The Last Year of Malcolm X by George Breitman, $14.95
Habla Malcolm X, $17.95

Order from Pathfinder

Also from Pathfinder

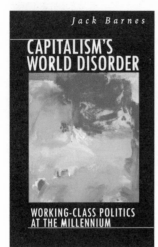

Capitalism's World Disorder
Working-Class Politics at the Millennium
JACK BARNES

The social devastation and financial panic, the coarsening of politics, the cop brutality and acts of imperialist aggression accelerating around us—all are the product not of something gone wrong but of the lawful workings of capitalism. Yet the future can be changed by the united struggle and selfless action of workers and farmers conscious of their power to transform the world. Also available in Spanish and French. $23.95

The Changing Face of U.S. Politics
Working-Class Politics and the Trade Unions
JACK BARNES

Building the kind of party the working class needs to prepare for coming class battles—battles through which they will revolutionize themselves, their unions, and all of society. It is a handbook for workers, farmers, and youth repelled by the class inequalities, economic instability, racism, women's oppression, cop violence, and wars endemic to capitalism, and who are seeking the road toward effective action to overturn that exploitative system and join in reconstructing the world on new, socialist foundations. Also available in Spanish and French. $23.00

The Communist Manifesto
KARL MARX AND FREDERICK ENGELS

Founding document of the modern working-class movement, published in 1848. Explains why communism is derived not from preconceived principles but from facts, from proletarian movements springing from the actual class struggle. Also available in Spanish. $3.95

Write for a catalog. See front of book for addresses.

The History of American Trotskyism, 1928–38

Report of a Participant

JAMES P. CANNON

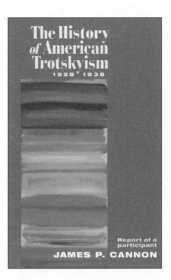

"Trotskyism is not a new movement, a new doctrine," Cannon says, "but the restoration, the revival of genuine Marxism as it was expounded and practiced in the Russian revolution and in the early days of the Communist International." In this series of twelve talks given in 1942, James P. Cannon recounts a decisive period in the efforts to build a proletarian party in the United States. Also in French and Spanish, $22.00

Their Trotsky and Ours

JACK BARNES

"History has shown that small revolutionary organizations will face not only the stern test of wars and repression, but also potentially shattering opportunities that emerge unexpectedly when strikes and social struggles explode. As that happens, communist parties not only recruit. They also fuse with other workers organizations and grow into mass proletarian parties contesting to lead workers and farmers to power. This assumes that well beforehand their cadres have absorbed a world communist program and strategy, are proletarian in life and work, derive deep satisfaction from—have fun—doing politics, and have forged a leadership with an acute sense of what to do next. *Their Trotsky and Ours* is about building such a party." $15.00

Maurice Bishop Speaks

The Grenada Revolution 1979–83

Speeches and interviews by the central leader of the workers and farmers government in the Caribbean island of Grenada. $24.95

U.S. Imperialism Has Lost the Cold War . . .

. . . That's what the Socialist Workers Party concluded a decade ago, in the wake of the collapse of regimes and parties across Eastern Europe and in the USSR that claimed to be Communist. Contrary to imperialism's hopes, the working class in those countries had not been crushed. It remains an intractable obstacle to reimposing and stabilizing capitalist relations, one that will have to be confronted by the exploiters in class battles—in a hot war.

Three issues of the Marxist magazine *New International* analyze the propertied rulers' failed expectations and chart a course for revolutionaries in response to the renewed rise of worker and farmer resistance to the economic and social instability, spreading wars, and rightist currents bred by the world market system. They explain why the historic odds in favor of the working class have increased, not diminished, at the opening of the 21st century.

New International no. 11

U.S. Imperialism Has Lost the Cold War *by Jack Barnes* • Socialism: A Viable Option *by José Ramón Balaguer* • Young Socialists Manifesto $14.00

New International no. 10

Imperialism's March toward Fascism and War *by Jack Barnes* • What the 1987 Stock Market Crash Foretold • Defending Cuba, Defending Cuba's Socialist Revolution *by Mary-Alice Waters* • The Curve of Capitalist Development *by Leon Trotsky* $14.00

New International no. 7

Opening Guns of World War III: Washington's Assault on Iraq *by Jack Barnes* • 1945: When U.S. Troops Said "No!" *by Mary-Alice Waters* • Lessons from the Iran-Iraq War *by Samad Sharif* $12.00

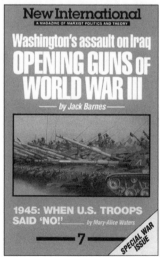

Distributed by Pathfinder

These issues of **New International** are also available in the Spanish **Nueva Internacional**, the French **Nouvelle Internationale**, and the Swedish **Ny International**.

African freedom struggle

HOW FAR WE SLAVES HAVE COME!
South Africa and Cuba in Today's World
NELSON MANDELA, FIDEL CASTRO

> Speaking together in Cuba in 1991, Mandela and Castro discuss the unique relationship and example of the struggles of the South African and Cuban peoples. $9.95

THOMAS SANKARA SPEAKS
The Burkina Faso Revolution 1983–87

> Peasants and workers in the West African country of Burkina Faso established a popular revolutionary government and began to combat the hunger, illiteracy, and economic backwardness imposed by imperialist domination. Thomas Sankara, who led that struggle, explains the example set for all of Africa. $19.95

WOMEN'S LIBERATION
AND THE AFRICAN FREEDOM STRUGGLE
THOMAS SANKARA

> "There is no true social revolution without the liberation of women," explains the leader of the 1983–87 revolution in Burkina Faso. $5.00

FROM THE ESCAMBRAY TO THE CONGO
In the Whirlwind of the Cuban Revolution
INTERVIEW WITH VICTOR DREKE

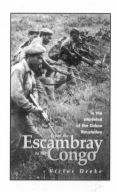

In this participant's account, Víctor Dreke describes how easy it became after the Cuban Revolution to take down the rope segregating blacks from whites at town dances, yet how enormous was the battle to transform social relations underlying all the "ropes" inherited from capitalism and Yankee domination. He recounts the determination, internationalism, and creative joy with which working people have defended their revolutionary course against U.S. imperialism from Cuba's own Escambray mountains, to the Americas, Africa, and beyond. $17.00

REVOLUTION IN THE CONGO
DICK ROBERTS

Describes the 1960 victory of Congolese peasants and workers, led by Patrice Lumumba, against Belgian colonial rule. And the role, under United Nations cover, of Washington, Brussels, and other imperialist powers in the overthrow and assassination of Lumumba. $3.00

NELSON MANDELA SPEAKS
Forging a Democratic, Nonracial South Africa
Speeches from 1990–93 recounting the struggle that put an end to apartheid and opened the fight for a deep-going political and social transformation in South Africa. $18.95

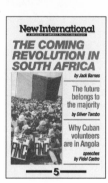

THE COMING REVOLUTION IN SOUTH AFRICA
JACK BARNES

Explores the social character and roots of apartheid in South African capitalism and the tasks of toilers in city and countryside in dismantling the legacy of class and racist inequality. Also includes "Why Cuban Volunteers Are in Angola," two speeches by Fidel Castro. In *New International* no. 5. $9.00

Further Reading

Lenin's Final Fight
Speeches and Writings, 1922–23
V.I. LENIN

In the early 1920s Lenin waged a
political battle in the Communist Party
leadership in the USSR to maintain the
course that had enabled workers and
peasants to overthrow the tsarist empire,
carry out the first socialist revolution, and
begin building a world communist
movement. The issues posed in this
fight—from the leadership's class
composition, to the worker-peasant
alliance and battle against national
oppression—remain central to world
politics today. $19.95. Also available in
Spanish.

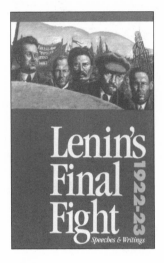

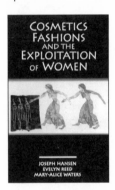

Cosmetics, Fashions, and the Exploitation of Women
JOSEPH HANSEN, EVELYN REED,
AND MARY-ALICE WATERS

How big business plays on women's second-
class status and social insecurities to market
cosmetics and rake in profits. The introduction by
Waters explains how the entry of millions of
women into the workforce during and after
World War II irreversibly changed U.S. society
and laid the basis for a renewed rise of struggles
for women's emancipation. $14.95

Fighting Racism in World War II
C.L.R. JAMES, GEORGE BREITMAN, EDGAR KEEMER,
AND OTHERS

A week-by-week account of the struggle against
lynch-mob terror and racist discrimination in U.S.
war industries, the armed forces, and society as
a whole from 1939 to 1945, taken from the
pages of the socialist newsweekly, the *Militant*.
These struggles helped lay the basis for the rise
of the mass civil rights movement in the
subsequent two decades. $21.95

From Pathfinder

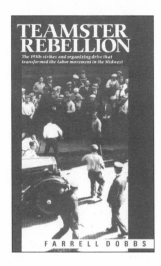

Teamster Rebellion

FARRELL DOBBS

The 1934 strikes that built the industrial union movement in Minneapolis and helped pave the way for the CIO, recounted by a central leader of that battle. The first in a four-volume series on the class-struggle leadership of the strikes and organizing drives that transformed the Teamsters union in much of the Midwest into a fighting social movement and pointed the road toward independent labor political action. $16.95

Socialism: Utopian and Scientific

FREDERICK ENGELS

Modern socialism is not a doctrine, Engels explains, but a working-class movement growing out of the establishment of large-scale capitalist industry and its social consequences. $4.00

The Revolution Betrayed

What Is the Soviet Union and Where Is It Going?

LEON TROTSKY

In 1917 the working class and peasantry of Russia were the motor force for one of the most profound revolutions in history. Yet within ten years a political counterrevolution by a privileged social layer whose chief spokesperson was Joseph Stalin was being consolidated. This classic study of the Soviet workers state and its degeneration illuminates the roots of the social and political crisis shaking the former Soviet Union today. $19.95

The Jewish Question

A Marxist Interpretation

ABRAM LEON

Traces the historical rationalizations of anti-Semitism to the fact that Jews—in the centuries preceding the domination of industrial capitalism—emerged as a "people-class" of merchants and moneylenders. Leon explains why the propertied rulers incite renewed Jew-hatred today. $17.95